ICAEW

Business, Technology and Finance

CW00376010

First edition 2007, Fifteenth edition 2021

ISBN 9781 5097 3844 1

British Library Cataloguing-in-Publication Data

A catalogue record for this book is available from the British Library

Published by

BPP Learning Media Ltd,
BPP House, Aldine Place,
142–144 Uxbridge Road,
London W12 8AA

www.bpp.com/learningmedia

Printed in the United Kingdom

©

BPP Learning Media Ltd
2021

Welcome to BPP Learning Media's ICAEW **Passcards** for **Business, Technology and Finance**.

- They **save you time**. Important topics are summarised for you.

- They incorporate **diagrams** to kick start your memory.

- They follow the overall **structure** of the ICAEW Workbook, but BPP Learning Media's ICAEW **Passcards** are not just a condensed book. Each card has been separately designed for clear presentation. Topics are self-contained and can be grasped visually.

- ICAEW **Passcards** are still **just the right size** for pockets, briefcases and bags.

- ICAEW **Passcards focus on the exams** you will be facing.

Run through the **Passcards** as often as you can during your final revision period. The day before the exam, try to go through the **Passcards** again! You will then be well on your way to passing your exams.

Good luck!

Contents

1: Introduction to business

This introduction to the 'business' element of the syllabus contains an overview of what a business is, who is interested in it and why, why it exists and what it sets out to do, and how the business knows whether it has succeeded.

Don't be tempted to regard this material as introductory but not examinable: the syllabus introduces the basics of many topics and the exam is there to make sure you know about them before you move on to further study of each topic.

Organisation

A **social arrangement** for **controlled performance** of **collective goals**, which has a **boundary** separating it from its environment.

→ Social arrangement = structure
→ Collective goals = **organisational objectives**
→ Controlled performance = monitoring, adjustment
→ Boundary = identity

Why do organisations exist?

- They overcome individuals' limitations
- They enable individuals to specialise
- They save time through joint effort
- They pool knowledge and ideas
- They pool expertise
- They enable synergy   2   +   2   =   5

Organisational objectives

- Market standing: eg, market share
- Innovation
- Productivity
- Physical and financial resources
- Profitability and wealth creation
- Manager performance and development
- Worker performance and attitude
- Social responsibility

Differences between organisations	**Areas of activity of industries**

Differences between organisations

- Ownership: private v public sector
- Control: by owners, manager or public servants
- Activity
- Orientation: profit v non-profit
- Size
- Legal status: sole trader, partnership or company
- Financing
- Technology

Areas of activity of industries

- Agriculture
- Extractive/raw materials } PRIMARY
- Manufacturing
- Energy production } SECONDARY
- Intellectual production
- Retailing/distribution
- Services } TERTIARY
- Technology

Business

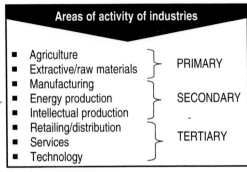

- Profit orientation = maximise owners' wealth
- Non-profit orientation = provide goods and services

An organisation that is oriented towards making a profit for its owners so as to maximise their wealth, and that can be regarded as an entity separate from its owners

Stakeholders

A person or group which has a stake in the business: an interest to protect

Stakeholder	Stake	Expectation
Primary		
Owners	Capital	Return on investment – dividend and capital growth
Secondary		
Directors/managers Employees	Livelihood, careers, and reputations	Remuneration, progression, stability and equity
Customers	Continued custom	Stability, quality and equity
Suppliers	Continued custom	Stability, payment and equity
Lenders	Capital	Return on investment – interest and repayment
Government/regulators	Infrastructure, welfare and tax revenue	Equity, investment
Public at large/natural environment	Infrastructure and environment	Protection

Business objectives

- Primary objective **eg** Maximisation of owners' wealth (profit)

TAKES PRECEDENCE OVER:

- Secondary objectives (support primary objective) **eg** Market position/share
  Product development
  Utilisation of technology
  Utilisation of labour resources
  Social responsibility

Alternative primary objectives may apply where:

- Managers lack a personal interest in wealth maximisation
- The business faces a lack of competition

- Profit satisficing
- Revenue maximisation
- Multiple objectives (Drucker)
- Constraints theory (Simon)

Hierarchy of objectives

Corporate objectives of firm as a whole
Take precedence over
Unit objectives for individual departments in the firm

Planning and control system

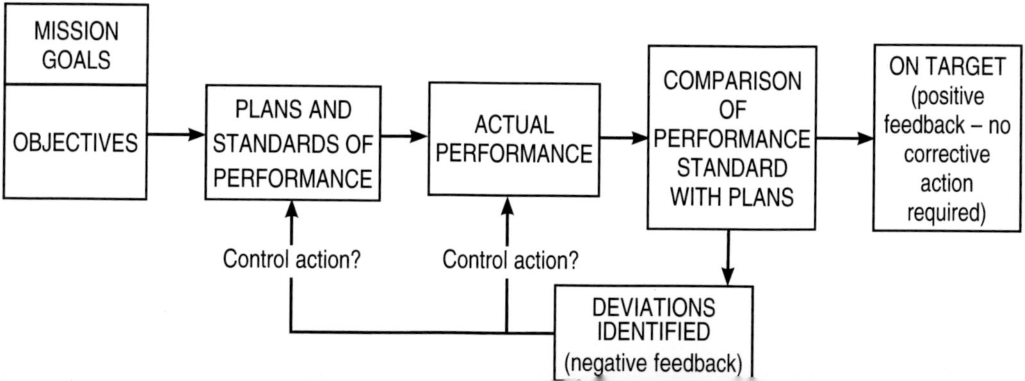

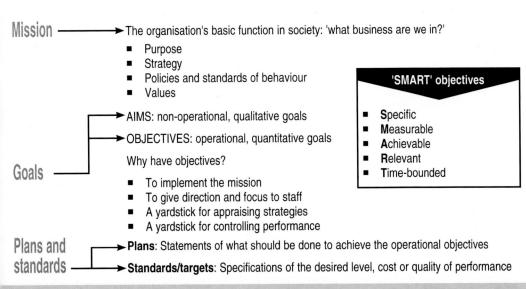

Mission ———→ The organisation's basic function in society: 'what business are we in?'

- Purpose
- Strategy
- Policies and standards of behaviour
- Values

→ AIMS: non-operational, qualitative goals

→ OBJECTIVES: operational, quantitative goals

Why have objectives?

- To implement the mission
- To give direction and focus to staff
- A yardstick for appraising strategies
- A yardstick for controlling performance

Goals

'SMART' objectives

- **S**pecific
- **M**easurable
- **A**chievable
- **R**elevant
- **T**ime-bounded

Plans and standards ——→ **Plans**: Statements of what should be done to achieve the operational objectives

→ **Standards/targets**: Specifications of the desired level, cost or quality of performance

Notes

2: Managing a business

Topic List

Management terms

Being a manager

Marketing management

Operations, procurement and HR management

Information technology

Organisational behaviour

In this rather lengthy chapter you need to appreciate a wide variety of terms, models and theories to do with how to manage a business day-to-day.

A business normally consists of several functions – finance, operations, marketing, IT and human resources – the first of which is the major focus of this exam. In this chapter however we look at the other functions, then at how people behave within the context of the organisation.

Management

Getting things done through other people

↓

Authority

The **right** of a person to ask someone else to do something and expect it to be done. Authority is conferred by the organisation

↑

Authority may be called 'position power' or 'legitimate power': it is power supported by the legal/ rational right to exercise it.

Responsibility

The obligation a person has to fulfil a task (s)he has been given, or to exercise authority in the interests of the organisation

Accountability

A person's liability to be called to account for the fulfilment of tasks or the exercise of authority: in effect, reporting back

What if authority ≠ responsibility?

- **Authority without responsibility** enables arbitrary, self-interested or irresponsible management.

- **Responsibility without authority** leads to frustration and stress.

A manager may **delegate** responsibility and authority to a subordinate to get a task done, but cannot delegate accountability for that task.

Managers using different levels of authority

Authority difficult to 'enforce': often regarded as interference

Difficult to balance with line managers' responsibilities

Line manager

Has direct authority over a subordinate in the scalar chain of command

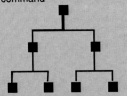

eg, department manager's authority over own staff

Staff manager

Has 'expert' influence, by which a manager or department has (limited) authority to advise another

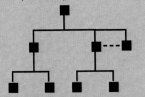

eg, an HR manager advising a department manager on selection techniques

Functional manager

Has 'expert' influence formalised as authority to direct or control relevant activities in line departments

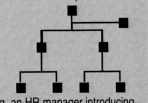

eg, an HR manager introducing equal opportunity policies to which line managers must adhere

2: Managing a business

Power The ability to get things done

Power is not necessarily conferred formally by the organisation, but can be derived (French & Raven, Charles Handy) from a number of sources of influence.

- **Coercive power**

  Physical force or threat of punishment: rare in organisations, but may be seen in intimidation tactics

- **Reward power**

  Control over the rewards and resources that people value: information, pay, status, facilities and so on

- **Position (legitimate) power**

  Power associated with (and legitimised by) a formal role and position in the organisation hierarchy, ie, 'authority'

- **Expert power**

  Control over knowledge, expertise or information that is recognised and valued by others

- **Personal (referent) power**

  Power associated with 'force of personality' or charisma – usually the result of high-level interpersonal skills (inspiring, influencing etc)

- **Negative power**

  The power to cause or threaten problems, costs, disruptions or other undesirable outcomes: the only power some members of the organisation may feel they have

The management hierarchy

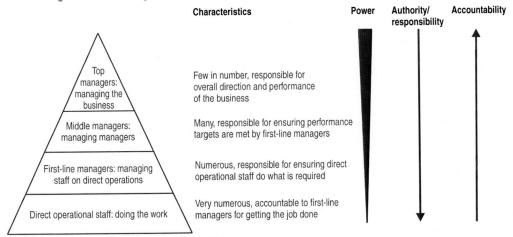

Characteristics

Top managers: managing the business
Few in number, responsible for overall direction and performance of the business

Middle managers: managing managers
Many, responsible for ensuring performance targets are met by first-line managers

First-line managers: managing staff on direct operations
Numerous, responsible for ensuring direct operational staff do what is required

Direct operational staff: doing the work
Very numerous, accountable to first-line managers for getting the job done

Power

Authority/ responsibility

Accountability

The management process

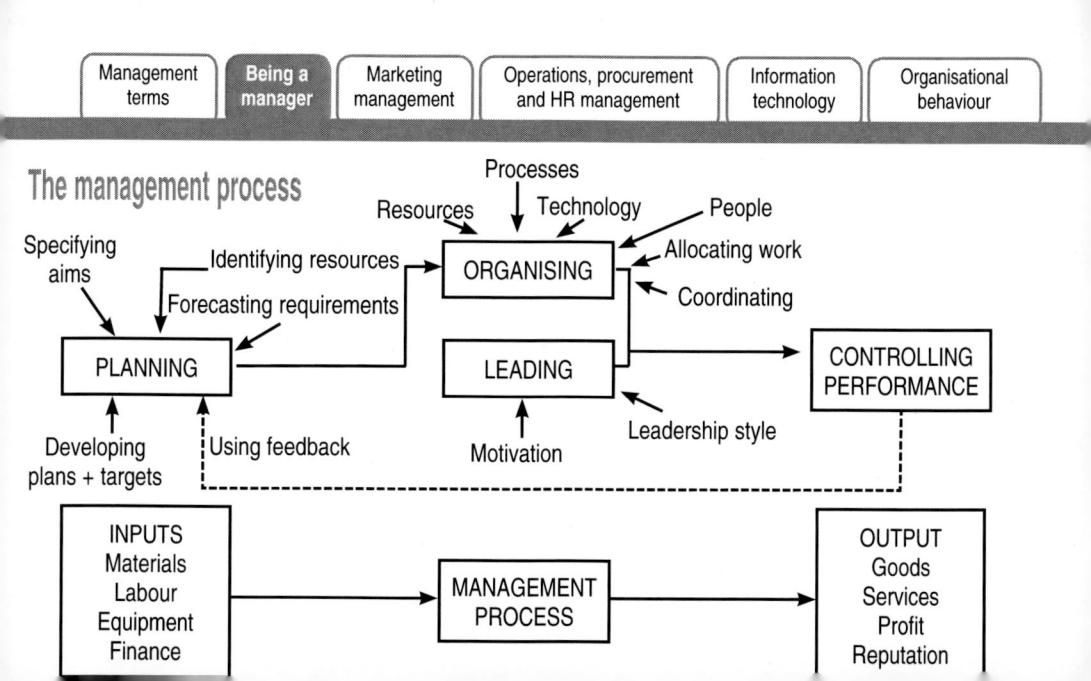

Managerial roles (Mintzberg)

Managers are not reflective, systematic planners: managerial work, in practice, is disjointed and discontinuous, and involves verbal/informal communication, intuition and judgement.

1	Interpersonal roles	■ Figurehead	A ceremonial role, representing the organisation
		■ Leader	Motivating, commanding, inspiring, developing staff
		■ Liaison	Maintaining contacts outside the vertical chain of command
2	Informational roles	■ Monitor	Scanning for information from internal and external networks
		■ Spokesperson	Providing information to interested parties on behalf of the organisation
		■ Disseminator	Sharing information via networks with those who need it
3	Decisional roles	■ Entrepreneur	Initiating projects, mobilising resources to meet opportunities
		■ Disturbance handler	Responding to pressures and problems that affect performance
		■ Resource allocator	Mobilising and allocating limited resources to teams/objectives
		■ Negotiator	Integrating different interests through bargaining processes
		■ Problem-solver	Resolving problems as they arise

2: Managing a business

| Management terms | Being a manager | Marketing management | Operations, procurement and HR management | Information technology | Organisational behaviour |

Culture and management (Quinn)

A business's culture – 'The way we see things round here' – affects how it is managed:

- Is flexibility or tight control more important?
- Does the business look inwards or outwards?

	+ FLEXIBLE		
+ INWARD-LOOKING	Human relations	Open systems	+ OUTWARD-LOOKING
	Internal process – **how** we do things	Rational goal – **why** we do things	
	+ CONTROL		

- Rational, systematic work methods
- Detailed rules, procedures and division of labour
- Hierarchical lines of authority
- Impersonality and low involvement employment relations
- Centralisation of planning and control

Business functions

- Marketing
- Operations
- Human resources
- Finance
- Information technology

Marketing

The management process which identifies, anticipates and supplies customer requirements efficiently and profitably

Consumer markets (B2C)

- Goods/services bought by individuals for their own or family use
- FMCGs: fast-moving consumer goods of low value, high volume eg, bread
- Consumer durables: white and brown goods, soft goods, and services

Industrial markets (B2B)

- Raw materials and components
- Capital goods
- Supplies
- Services

Market segmentation

Subdividing a market into increasingly homogeneous subgroups of customers, any subgroup can be selected as a **target market** to be met with a distinct **marketing mix**

Based upon

- Geographic area
- Age
- Household status
- Religion/ethnicity
- Social class/lifestyle

Target market

One or more segments selected for special attention by a company

Segments should be

- Measurable
- Accessible
- The right size
- Potentially profitable
- Susceptible to a distinct marketing mix

Management terms	Being a manager	Marketing management	Operations, procurement and HR management	Information technology	Organisational behaviour

Marketing mix

The set of controllable variables and their levels that the firm uses to influence the target market. These elements are interdependent

The elements must be in **balance**

4Ps

Product

The product is a **package of benefits** that meets a need or provides a solution. The **core product** consists of the essential features; the **augmented product** provides additional benefits

⬇

Important factors

- Quality and reliability
- Packaging
- Branding
- Aesthetics
- Product mix
- Servicing
- Technology

Place

Distribution (or outlets) and **logistics** support the overall marketing effort by providing the promised customer satisfactions

⬇

Important factors

- Availability
- Location
- Timing
- Sell direct?
- Use intermediaries? (retailers, wholesalers)

Promotion

Communicating benefits to customers

Important factors	
■ Advertising	■ Push or pull techniques?
■ Sales promotions	■ Digital marketing
■ Public relations	
■ Personal selling	

Price

Pricing includes discounts and credit terms. It is influenced by costs, which must be covered, by demand and its elasticity, and by the competition. It is very closely related to promotion and brand/ product image

Operations management and procurement

Creating as required the goods or services supplied to customers

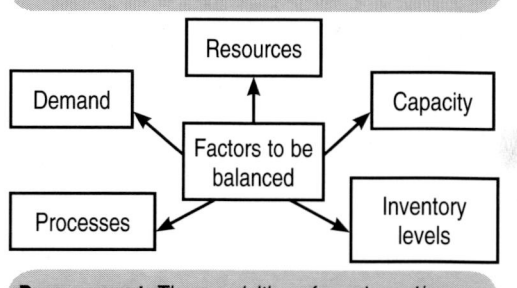

Procurement: The acquisition of goods and/or services at the best possible total cost of ownership, in the right quantity and quality, at the right time, in the right place and from the right source for the direct benefit or use of the business

Human resource management

Creating, developing and maintaining an effective workforce, matching business requirements and responding to the environment

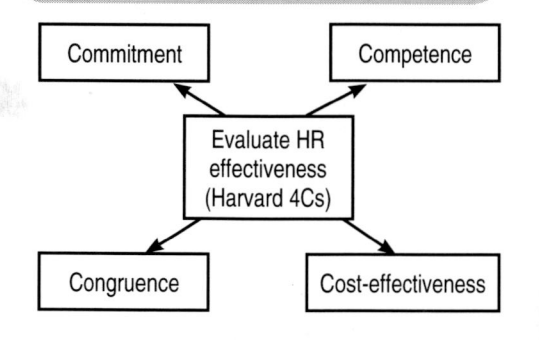

Information technology

The ICAEW's Information Technology Faculty guide *Managing SME: A guide for Finance Directors* states that "The mission for the IT function is to add persistent value, through the effective application of appropriate technology". The following table summarises some of the advice that the guide provides in regard to managing an IT function:

Management action	Advice
Monitoring	IT developments are often rapid and difficult to keep up-to-date with. Companies whose finance directors are unaware of them could be missing out on opportunities to develop the business and its systems for the better. Therefore it is vital to maintain an awareness of potentially useful developments and any compliance obligations, by building up a list of contacts and information sources which can be turned to from time-to-time. Examples of such developments include cloud computing, automation and intelligent systems which we shall look at in Chapter 6.
Planning	IT functions and the effective management of change require careful planning and preparation to ensure everything runs smoothly and without disruption.
Structure	IT management tasks should be prioritised and documented. There should be a rolling programme of 'business as usual' and 'forward change' activities.
Staffing and skills	IT teams require the right people to be recruited and retained. This means employing staff with suitable skills and experience in data science (see Chapter 6) and matching them to the most appropriate roles.

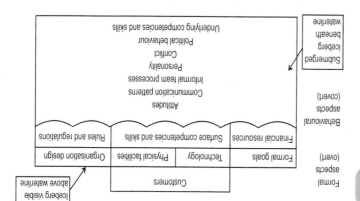

Organisational behaviour

Individual and group behaviour in an organisational setting

Organisational iceberg

Formal aspects (overt)

- Formal goals
- Financial resources
- Technology
- Physical facilities
- Surface competencies and skills
- Organisation design
- Rules and regulations
- Customers

Iceberg visible above waterline

Behavioural aspects (covert)

- Attitudes
- Communication patterns
- Informal team processes
- Personality
- Conflict
- Political behaviour
- Underlying competencies and skills

Submerged iceberg beneath waterline

Motivation

Needs ➝ goals and strategies ➝ behaviour

Hierarchy of needs (Maslow)

- Self-actualisation – Fulfilment of personal potential
- Esteem needs – For independence, recognition, status, respect from others
- Social needs – For relationships, affection, belonging
- Safety needs – For security, order, predictability, freedom from threat
- Physiological needs – Food, shelter

2: Managing a business

Groups

Any collection of people who see themselves as a group

- Common aim or purpose
- A sense of identity
- Existence of group norms
- Internal communication
- Leadership

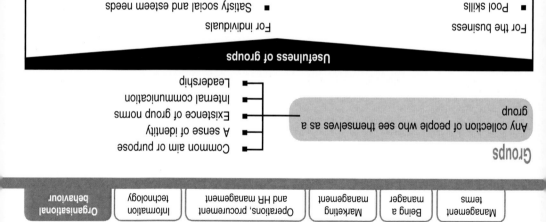

Usefulness of groups

For the business

- Pool skills
- Plan and organise
- Solve problems/take decisions
- Distribute information
- Co-ordinate between departments

For individuals

- Satisfy social and esteem needs
- Give support
- Provide social contact and personal relationships

Stages of group development (Tuckman)

1 FORMING — The group is coming together. Individuals try to find out about each other and the aims and norms of the group.

2 STORMING — Aims, procedures and roles (including leadership) begin to be hammered out through more or less open conflict.

3 NORMING — The group begins to settle down, reaching agreements on work-sharing, roles and norms. Group decision-making begins.

4 PERFORMING — The group is ready to set to work on its task: the process of formation no longer absorbs attention. The focus shifts to results.

Group roles (Belbin)

1 **Leader:** presides over team activity (balanced, disciplined, good at working through others)

2 **Shaper:** spurs the team on to action (dominant, extrovert, passionate about the task)

3 **Plant:** provides the team with ideas, proposals (introverted but creatively intelligent)

4 **Evaluator:** dissects and criticises ideas: spots potential problems (analytically intelligent)

5 **Resource-investigator:** accesses new contacts and resources (extrovert networker; not an originator)

6 **Company worker:** translates ideas into practice, plans (not a leader, but an essential organiser)

7 **Team-worker:** holds the team together, supports members (empathetic, diplomatic)

8 **Finisher:** chivvies the team to attend to details/deadlines/follow-up

9 **Specialist:** outsider

The effective manager

Participative continuum (Likert)

Influences
■ Extent of authority
■ Amount of autonomy given to subordinates
■ Leadership 'style'

Characteristics (Likert)
■ Encourages participation
■ Employee-centred rather than work-centred
■ Has high standards but is flexible re methods
■ Natural delegator; trusting

Exploitative – authoritative	Benevolent – authoritative	Consultative	Participative
Decisions imposed	Increasing trust in subordinates' ability		Complete trust + discussion
Motivated by threats	More participative motivation style		Motivated by rewards – goals agreed
Centralised decision-making	Increasing delegation		High degree of delegation
Little superior/ subordinate communication	Increasing communication		Frequent communication
Superior + subordinates act as individuals – no teamwork	Increasing teamwork		Superior + subordinates act as a team

Delegation

The process whereby a superior passes to a subordinate part of his or her own responsibility and authority to make decisions.

Remember: The delegator is still **accountable** to his or her superior for the results of delegated decisions

Advantages of delegation

- ☑ Facilitates career development/succession planning
- ☑ Manager freed from less important activities
- ☑ Enables relevant and speedy decision-making
- ☑ Enhances flexibility
- ☑ Makes subordinate's job more interesting
- ☑ Motivational

Problems of poor delegation

- ☒ Insufficient skills/training
- ☒ Too much supervision wastes time
- ☒ Too little leads to poor performance
- ☒ 'Passing the buck'
- ☒ Only boring or impossible work is delegated
- ☒ Fear by manager of losing control

3: Organisational and business structures

Topic List

Principles of organisational structure

Types of organisational structure

Centralisation and decentralisation

Tall and flat organisations

Span of control

Bureaucracy

Business forms

In this chapter we cover how a business of any size is structured, and its various parts co-ordinated. We also look at the various types of legal structure that may be adopted.

Formal organisation structure

Links individuals in a network of reporting relationships and communication lines. It groups and allocates tasks, defines authority, and links and shapes the co-ordinated flow of work, information and resources through the organisation

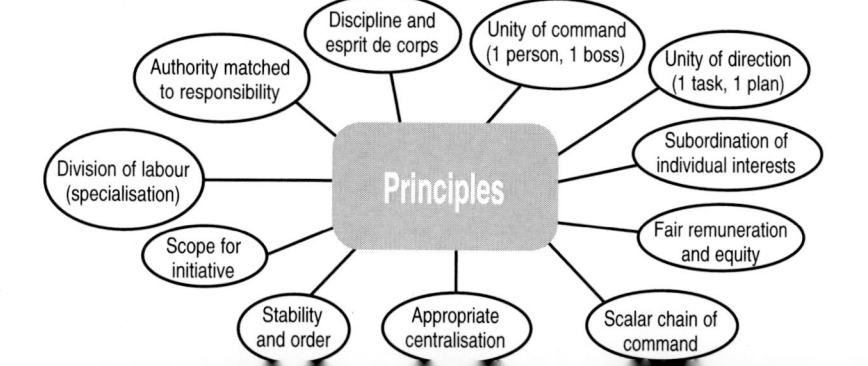

Building blocks and coordinating mechanisms (Mintzberg)

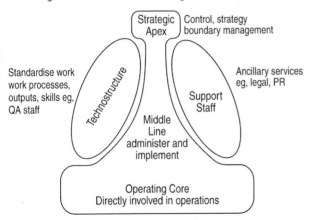

Strategic Apex — Control, strategy boundary management

Technostructure — Standardise work work processes, outputs, skills eg, QA staff

Support Staff — Ancillary services eg, legal, PR

Middle Line administer and implement

Operating Core Directly involved in operations

Processes by which work is coordinated

- Mutual adjustment
- Direct supervision
- Standardisation of work processes
- Standardisation of outputs (by performance measures)
- Standardisation of skills and knowledge

3: Organisational and business structures

The business's external environment affects its structure

Structure environment
- Structure – slow environmental change
- Single product/market
- Simple technology
- Safe

Dynamic environment
- Dynamic – rapid, accelerating change
- Diverse – international, many products and markets
- Difficult – analysis is not easy
- Dangerous

| Principles of organisational structure | Types of organisational structure | Centralisation and decentralisation | Tall and flat organisations | Span of control |

Types of business structure	External environment	Internal factors	Key building block	Key co-ordinating mechanism
Simple entrepreneurial structure	Simple Dynamic	Small Young Simple tasks	Strategic apex	Direct supervision
Machine bureaucracy/ functional structure	Simple Static	Large Old Regulated	Technostructure	Standardisation of work
Professional bureaucracy	Complex Static	Professional Simple systems	Operating core	Standardisation of skills
Divisional structure	Simple Static Diverse	Very large Old Divisible tasks	Middle line	Standardisation of outputs
Advocacy/ innovative/matrix	Complex Dynamic	Young Complex tasks	Operating core	Mutual adjustment

3: Organisational and business structures

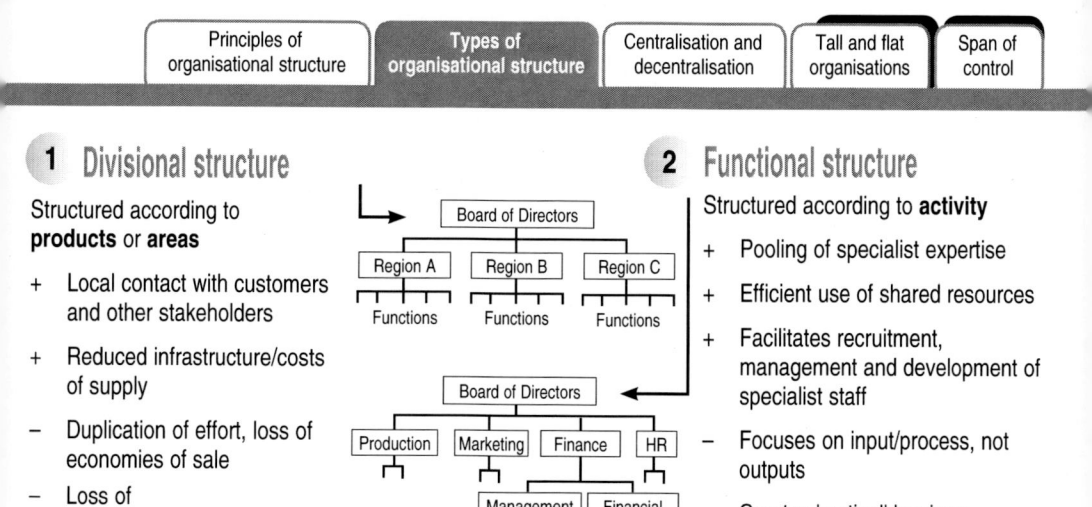

1 Divisional structure

Structured according to **products** or **areas**

- \+ Local contact with customers and other stakeholders

- \+ Reduced infrastructure/costs of supply

- − Duplication of effort, loss of economies of sale

- − Loss of consistency/standardisation

2 Functional structure

Structured according to **activity**

- \+ Pooling of specialist expertise

- \+ Efficient use of shared resources

- \+ Facilitates recruitment, management and development of specialist staff

- − Focuses on input/process, not outputs

- − Creates 'vertical' barriers: impedes workflow, coordination, communication, growth, diversification

Board of Directors

Region A | Region B | Region C

Functions | Functions | Functions

Board of Directors

Production | Marketing | Finance | HR

Management Accountant | Financial Accountant

3 Matrix structure

This is a form of organisation which 'crosses' functional and divisional structures, forming multi-functional units (or teams), under the control of a product or project manager. Team members also report to their line manager on day-to-day operations.

	Production	Sales	Finance	IT	R & D	Marketing
Product Manager A						
Project Manager B						
Area Manager C						

+ Facilitates flexibility

+ Abolishes vertical boundaries

+ Pools multi-functional expertise

+ Involves people in the big picture

– Threatens managerial conflict

– Can be stressful for employees

– May add costs of managerial complexity and co-ordination

| Principles of organisational structure | Types of organisational structure | **Centralisation and decentralisation** | Tall and flat organisations | Span of control |

Centralisation

Refers to the concentration of authority in one place:
- Geographically
- In the hierarchy of authority

Arguments pro centralisation

- Decisions easier to control and coordinate
- Senior managers have access to the 'big picture'
- Senior managers can balance demands of different functions
- Decisions may benefit from senior managers' experience/contacts
- May reduce overheads (fewer managerial salaries)
- Crisis decisions can be taken speedily (no reference)
- Policy decisions can be standardised organisation wide

Decentralisation

Refers to the delegation or devolution of authority:
- To local business units
- To lower levels of the hierarchy

Arguments pro decentralisation

- Avoids overburdening senior managers with detail
- Improves motivation of subordinates given responsibility
- Decision makers are more aware of local/front-line issues
- Greater speed of decision-making (less reference upwards)
- Facilitates development/succession of junior managers
- More distinct areas of accountability for controls
- Supported by communications and information technology
- More flexible in the face of customer demands

Tall organisation	Flat organisation
✓ Narrow control spans → managerial control	✓ Strategic apex close to operating core
✓ Defined career ladder → employee loyalty	✓ Strategic apex close to the customer
✓ Specialisation → technical excellence	✓ Savings on managerial costs
✗ Close control fosters rigidity, blocks initiative	✓ More opportunity for delegation/empowerment
✗ Increased administration and overhead costs	✗ Loss of managerial control
✗ Lengthens communication and decision-making	✗ Loss of middle management interface
✗ Strategic apex distanced from the customer	✗ If delayered, loss of middle management knowledge

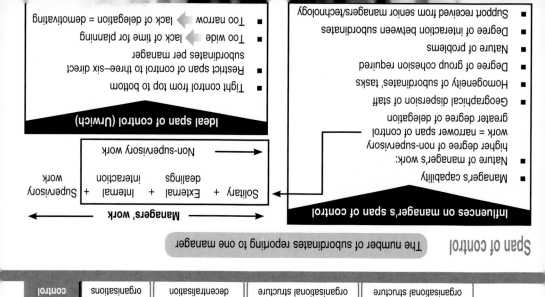

Span of control

Principles of organisational structure | Types of organisational structure | Centralisation and decentralisation | Tall and flat organisations | **Span of control**

The number of subordinates reporting to one manager

Managers' work

Solitary + External + Internal dealings + interaction + Supervisory work

Non-supervisory work

Supervisory work ← → Managers' work

Influences on manager's span of control

- Manager's capability
- Nature of manager's work:
  higher degree of non-supervisory
  work = narrower span of control →
  greater degree of delegation
- Geographical dispersion of staff
- Homogeneity of subordinates' tasks
- Degree of group cohesion required
- Nature of problems
- Degree of interaction between subordinates
- Support received from senior managers/technology

Ideal span of control (Urwich)

- Tight control from top to bottom
- Restrict span of control to three–six direct subordinates per manager
- Too wide = lack of time for planning
- Too narrow = lack of delegation = demotivating

Bureaucracy

→ Very stable, predictable

A 'continuous organisation of official functions bound by rules.' (Weber)

Efficient, safe
Technical competence ← Impersonal, rational, fair ←
← Hierarchical, specialised ←

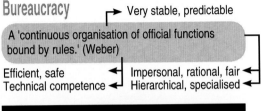

Characteristics of bureaucracy

- Hierarchy of roles
- Specialisation/need for training
- Professional nature of employment
- Impersonal nature
- Rationality
- Uniformity in performance of tasks
- Technical competence
- Stability

Problems with bureaucracy

☒ Slow communication and decision making
☒ Conformity (while 'safe') can inhibit growth, development
☒ Rigidity of rules leads to inability to change, adapt
☒ Restricted communication inhibits innovation
☒ Lack of feedback leads to inability to learn from mistakes

└─ (Burns & Stalker) 'Mechanistic organisation'

3: Organisational and business structures

Sole trader

Owns the business alone, taking all the risks and rewards

Features of sole trader

- No separation of identity between owner and business
- Unlimited liability of sole trader for business debts
- Finance: capital introduced + retained earnings + loans + short term credit
- Security for loans: fixed, not floating, charge
- Drawings
- May employ staff
- Sole tradership ceases on death

+ Flexible
+ No publicity
− Sole responsibility for everything

Partnership

The relationship which exists between two or more persons carrying on a business in common with a view of profit.

Features of partnership

- Similar to sole trading; two sole traders
- Terms of agreement between partners are very important
- General partnerships (unlimited joint + several liability) are most common

+ Flexible
+ No publicity
+ Share skills, and responsibility
+ New ideas and capital
− Importance of trust between partners

Features of a limited company

- ☑ Company is legally distinct from its owners (members)
- ☑ Members' liability for company's debts is limited to the amount unpaid, if any, on their shares
- ☒ Separation of ownership (members) and control (directors)
- ☒ Shareholders take dividends declared by directors
- ☑ Shares are a form of property that can be transferred easily
- ☑ Perpetual succession on members' death
- ☑ Can give floating as well as fixed charges
- ☒ Shareholders do not own assets; company does
- ☒ Publicity (financial statements and filing information)
- ☒ Regulation and expense

Joint ventures

Arrangements between businesses to pool their interests on a project. The mechanism is usually a subsidiary company

Strategic alliances

Tend to be for the longer term and aim to complement technology, geography, markets and so on

Other co-operative methods

- **Licensing** – the licenser provides rights, advice and know how in return for a royalty
- **Franchising** – the franchiser provides expertise and brand, the franchisee provides capital
- **Sub-contracting** – enhanced access to resources, reduce overheads
- **Agents** – used as a distribution network

Advantages of alliances

☑ Coverage of a larger number of markets
☑ Reduced risk of government intervention
☑ Closer control over operations
☑ Local knowledge
☑ Spreading of risk and costs
☑ Learning from partners

Conflicts

- Profit sharing
- Investment levels
- Management
- Marketing strategy

4: Introduction to business strategy

Topic List

What is strategy?

Strategic planning process

External analysis

Internal analysis

Corporate appraisal

Mission, goals and objectives

Strategic options and choice

This substantial chapter covers the key elements of the strategic planning process, including many models which are highly examinable.

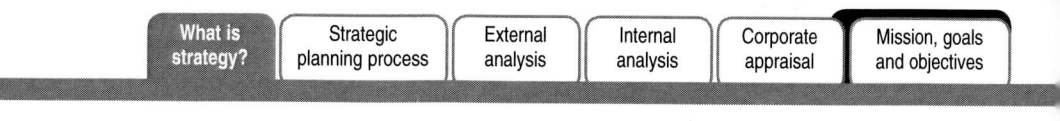

Planning

The establishment of objectives, and those policies, strategies, tactics and actions required to achieve them

is the basis for

Managing business strategy

Strategy: Course of action to achieve a specific objective

Strategic plan: Statement of long term goals, and those policies which will ensure their achievement

Strategic management: Management of the elements involved in planning and controlling a business strategy: taking decisions about the business's scope and long-term future, and allocating resources

Level of strategy reflects the divisionalised business

Corporate strategy

Overall control of resources, setting of mission, objectives and values: looks at the longest timescale, at major products/markets and investment and financing decisions

↓

Strategic plan
and master budget

Business strategy

The approach to competition and marketing in a particular product market: strategy at the SBU level, including the marketing mix (competitive strategy), the balance of projects (investment strategy) and the finance required (financial strategy)

↓

Business plans
and budgets

Functional operational strategy

Planning the work of a functional specialisation such as marketing, operations, HR and finance

↓

Operational plans and budgets

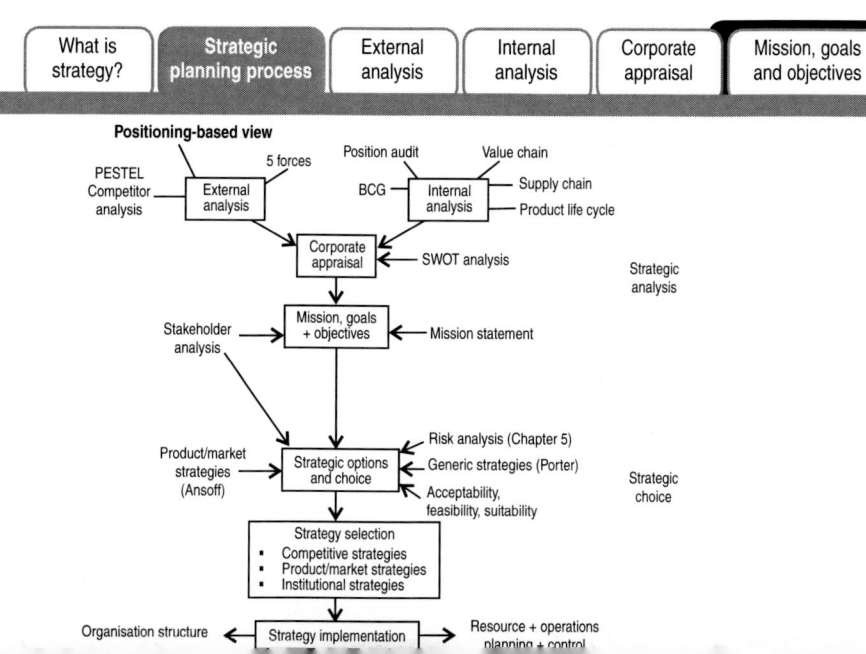

The business must analyse its external general and task environment

General environment

Includes political, legal, economic, social, ecological and technological factors (PESTEL)

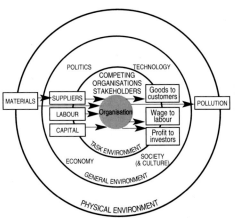

Task environment

Includes factors of particular relevance to the business, such as competitors, suppliers and customers

PESTEL analysis

Political factors

- Capacity expansion
- Demand
- Divestment/rationalisation
- Emerging industries
- Entry barriers
- Competition

Legal factors

- Legal framework: contract, tort, agency
- Criminal law
- Company law
- Employment
- Health and Safety
- Data and consumer protection
- Environment
- Tax law

Economic factors

- Local economic trends: working population and skills, cost of living
- Inflation
- Interest rates
- Tax levels
- Government spending
- Business cycle
- Productivity

Government policy

- Fiscal policy (taxes, borrowing, spending)
- Monetary policy (interest rates, exchange rates)
- Size and scope of the public sector
- Regulation

Social factors – demography	Technological factors	Ecological factors
■ Growth ■ Age ■ Geography ■ Household structure ■ Social structure ■ Employment ■ Wealth	■ Rate of change ■ Types of product/service ■ Production, materials/equipment/processes ■ Information storage, management, analysis and communication ■ Cyber risk	■ Resources ■ Waste ■ Regulation ■ Disasters ■ Demand ■ Pressure groups ■ Natural capital

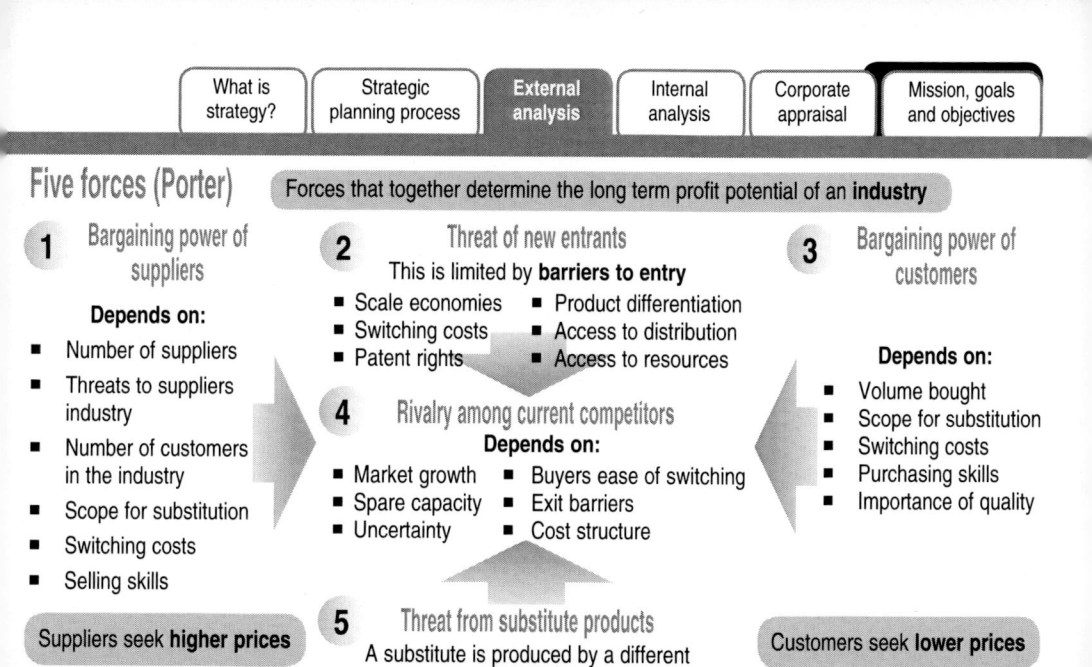

Five forces (Porter)

Forces that together determine the long term profit potential of an **industry**

1 Bargaining power of suppliers

Depends on:

- Number of suppliers
- Threats to suppliers industry
- Number of customers in the industry
- Scope for substitution
- Switching costs
- Selling skills

Suppliers seek **higher prices**

2 Threat of new entrants

This is limited by **barriers to entry**

- Scale economies
- Product differentiation
- Switching costs
- Access to distribution
- Patent rights
- Access to resources

4 Rivalry among current competitors

Depends on:

- Market growth
- Buyers ease of switching
- Spare capacity
- Exit barriers
- Uncertainty
- Cost structure

3 Bargaining power of customers

Depends on:

- Volume bought
- Scope for substitution
- Switching costs
- Purchasing skills
- Importance of quality

Customers seek **lower prices**

5 Threat from substitute products

A substitute is produced by a different industry but satisfies the same needs

Competitor analysis

Types of competitor (Kotler)

- Brand: McDonald's v Burger King
- Industry: online retailing v traditional retailing
- Generic: music downloads v Netflix
- Form: matches v cigarette lighters

For each competitor analyse

- Its strategy, including its structure and purpose
- Its assumptions about the industry
- Its current and potential situation
- Its capability
- Its reaction profile
  - Laid back
  - Tiger
  - Selective
  - Stochastic

Position audit

Examination of the business's current state in terms of resources and competencies

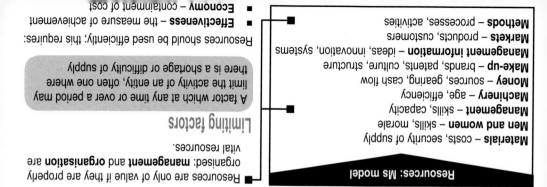

Resources: Ms model

Materials – costs, security of supply
Men and women – skills, morale
Management – skills, capacity
Machinery – age, efficiency
Money – sources, gearing, cash flow
Make-up – brands, patents, culture, structure
Management information – ideas, innovation, systems
Markets – products, customers
Methods – processes, activities

- Resources are only of value if they are properly organised: **management** and **organisation** are vital resources.

Limiting factors

A factor which at any time or over a period may limit the activity of an entity, often one where there is a shortage or difficulty of supply

Resources should be used efficiently; this requires:

- **Effectiveness** – the measure of achievement
- **Economy** – containment of cost

Value chain (Porter)

SUPPORT ACTIVITIES	FIRM INFRASTRUCTURE	MARGIN
	HUMAN RESOURCE MANAGEMENT	
	TECHNOLOGY DEVELOPMENT	
	PROCUREMENT	
	INBOUND LOGISTICS / OPERATIONS / OUTBOUND LOGISTICS / MARKETING & SALES / SERVICE	MARGIN
	PRIMARY ACTIVITIES	

A firm's value chain is connected to what **Porter** calls a **value system**.

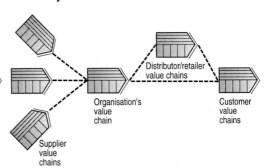

Supplier value chains

Organisation's value chain

Distributor/retailer value chains

Customer value chains

Margin

This is the excess the customer is prepared to **pay** over the **cost** to the firm of obtaining resource inputs and providing value activities. It represents the **value created** by the **value activities** themselves and by the **management of the linkages** between them. **Linkages** connect the activities in the value chain. The activities affect one another and therefore must be co-ordinated.

How to secure a competitive advantage

- Invent new or better ways to do activities
- Combine activities in new or better ways
- Manage the linkages in its own value chain
- Manage the linkages in the value system

Supply chain

A **network between businesses**, rather than a **pipeline**, of close links and greater co-operation

Supply chain management

Optimising the activities of businesses working together to produce goods and services

Suppliers

This can be achieved via

- Reduction in number of suppliers partnering
- Reduction in number of customers
- Price and inventory co-ordination
- Linked computer systems
- Early supplier involvement in product development and design
- Logistics design
- Joint problem solving
- Supplier representative on site

Customers

Product life cycle

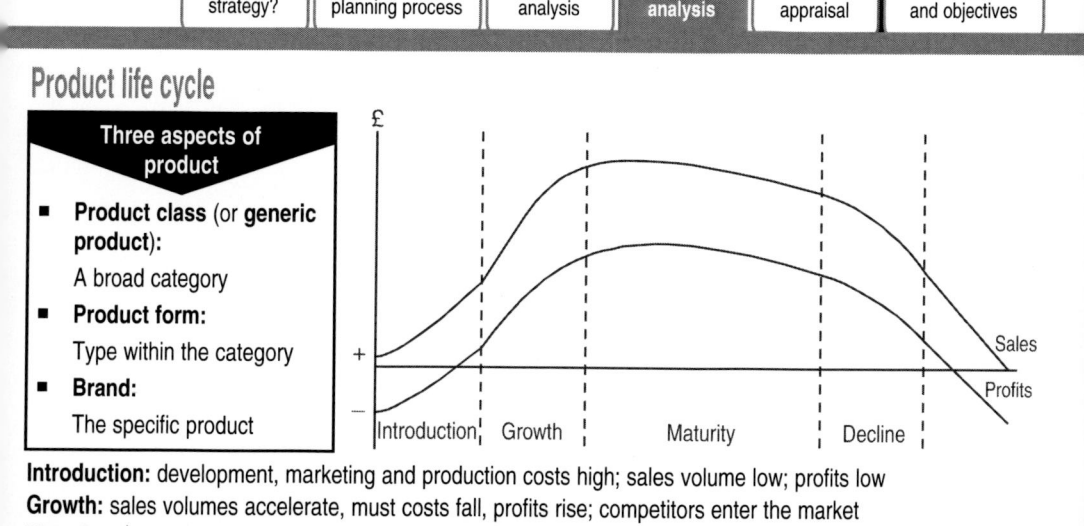

Three aspects of product

- **Product class** (or **generic product**):
  A broad category
- **Product form**:
  Type within the category
- **Brand**:
  The specific product

Introduction: development, marketing and production costs high; sales volume low; profits low
Growth: sales volumes accelerate, must costs fall, profits rise; competitors enter the market
Maturity: longest period; profits good, reminder promotion
Decline: many causes; sales fall, overcapacity in industry; some players leave market

BCG matrix

Applicable to products, market segments and SBUs

Four strategies
1 **Build**: Invest for market share growth
2 **Hold**: Maintain current position
3 **Harvest**: Manage for profit in the short term
4 **Divest**: Release resources for use elsewhere

The BCG Matrix

Market growth			
	High	Star	Question mark
	Low	Cash cow	Dog
		High	Low

Market share relative to largest competitor

Stars – build
Cash cows – hold or harvest
Question marks – hold or harvest
Dogs – divest or hold

Corporate appraisal

Draws together the internal and external assessments in an analysis of strengths, weaknesses, opportunities and threats (SWOT analysis). A good strategy will utilise strengths to exploit opportunities while evading threats and minimising the effect of weaknesses.

SWOT analysis

A review of:

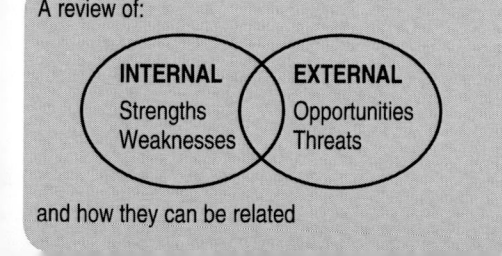

and how they can be related

The results can be combined in the SWOT framework.

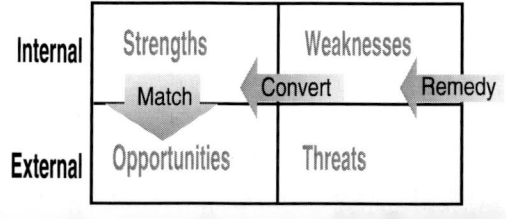

Stakeholder analysis (Mendelow)

Stakeholders' interests are likely to conflict. **Mendelow's stakeholder analysis** helps the business identify the key stakeholders and their sources of power when setting missions, goals and objectives.

Level of interest

- **A**: Minimal effort
- **B**: **Keep informed**; little direct influence but may influence more powerful stakeholders
- **C**: Treat with care; often passive but capable of moving to segment D; **keep satisfied**
- **D**: **Key players** – strategy must be **acceptable** to them, at least

Hierarchy of objectives and strategies (top-down)

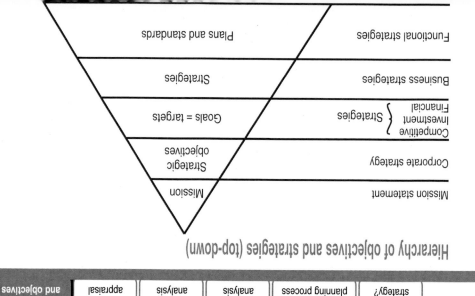

Mission statement	Mission
Corporate strategy	Strategic objectives
Strategies { Competitive, Investment, Financial }	Goals = targets
Business strategies	Strategies
Functional strategies	Plans and standards

Mission statement

'The organisation's basic function in society' (**Mintzberg**)

Includes

- Purpose
- Basic strategy eg, products
- Policies and standards of behaviour
- Values and culture
  - Business principles
  - Internal relationships
  - Behaviour

A formal **mission statement** may:

- Impress customers
- Motivate staff
- Guide manager's actions
- Guide strategic thinking

BUT it may also:

- Be ignored in practice
- Be treated cynically as mere PR
- Merely rationalise what is done anyway
- Be the same as everyone else's

Strategic objectives and corporate strategy

The primary objective – maximising shareholder wealth – plus other major objectives arising from stakeholder analysis, formulated as **corporate strategy**

| Competitive strategy | Investment strategy | Financial strategy |

Generic strategies and the five competitive forces (Porter)

- **Cost leadership** – producing at lowest cost in the industry
- **Differentiation** – providing a unique product/service
- **Focus/niche** – restricting activities to a segment using either a cost leadership or a differentiation-focus

Competitive force	Cost leadership	Differentiation
New entrants	+ Economies of scale raise entry barriers	+ Brand loyalty and perceived uniqueness are entry barriers
Substitutes	+ Firm is not so vulnerable as its less cost-effective competitors to the threat of substitutes	+ Customer loyalty is a weapon against substitutes
Customers	+ Customers cannot drive down prices further than the next most efficient competitor	+ Customers have no comparable alternative + Brand loyalty should lower price sensitivity − Customers may no longer need the differentiating factor − Sooner or later, customers become price sensitive
Suppliers	+ Flexibility to deal with cost increases − Higher margins can offset vulnerability to supplier price rises	+ Increase in input costs can reduce price advantages
Industry rivalry	+ Firms remains profitable when rivals go under through excessive price competition − Technological change will require capital investment, or make production cheaper for competitors − Competitors learn via imitation − Cost concerns ignore product design or marketing issues	+ Unique features reduce direct competition − Imitation narrows differentiation

Product/market strategies (Ansoff)

Ansoff described the four possible growth vectors in the four cells in the diagram below. Numbers in circles show relative riskiness.

	Product Existing	**Product** New
Market Existing	**Market penetration** ① ■ Maintain or increase market share ■ Dominate growth markets ■ Drive out competition from mature markets ■ Increase usage by existing customers	**Product development** ③ ■ Launch new products ■ May require new competences ■ Forces competitors to follow suit ■ Discourages newcomers ■ Expensive
Market New	**Market development** ② ■ New markets for current products ■ New geographic areas – export ■ New package sizes ■ New distribution channels ■ Differential pricing to suit new segments	**Diversification** ④ Related — Unrelated (conglomerate) Vertical Horizontal Forward Backward New **competences** will be required

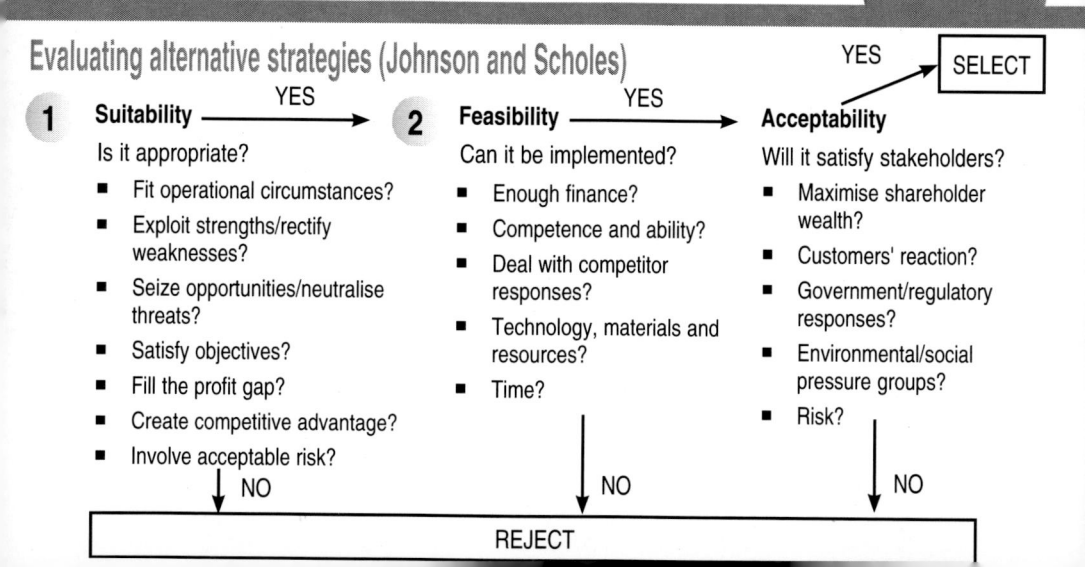

Evaluating alternative strategies (Johnson and Scholes)

1 **Suitability** ——YES——> **2** **Feasibility** ——YES——> **Acceptability** ——YES——> SELECT

Suitability

Is it appropriate?

- Fit operational circumstances?
- Exploit strengths/rectify weaknesses?
- Seize opportunities/neutralise threats?
- Satisfy objectives?
- Fill the profit gap?
- Create competitive advantage?
- Involve acceptable risk?

Feasibility

Can it be implemented?

- Enough finance?
- Competence and ability?
- Deal with competitor responses?
- Technology, materials and resources?
- Time?

Acceptability

Will it satisfy stakeholders?

- Maximise shareholder wealth?
- Customers' reaction?
- Government/regulatory responses?
- Environmental/social pressure groups?
- Risk?

NO ↓   NO ↓   NO ↓

REJECT

5: Introduction to risk management

Risk analysis is part of the strategic planning process, and risk is also an important element in working capital management and in corporate governance.

In this chapter we introduce what is meant by the term 'risk', and how it can be managed.

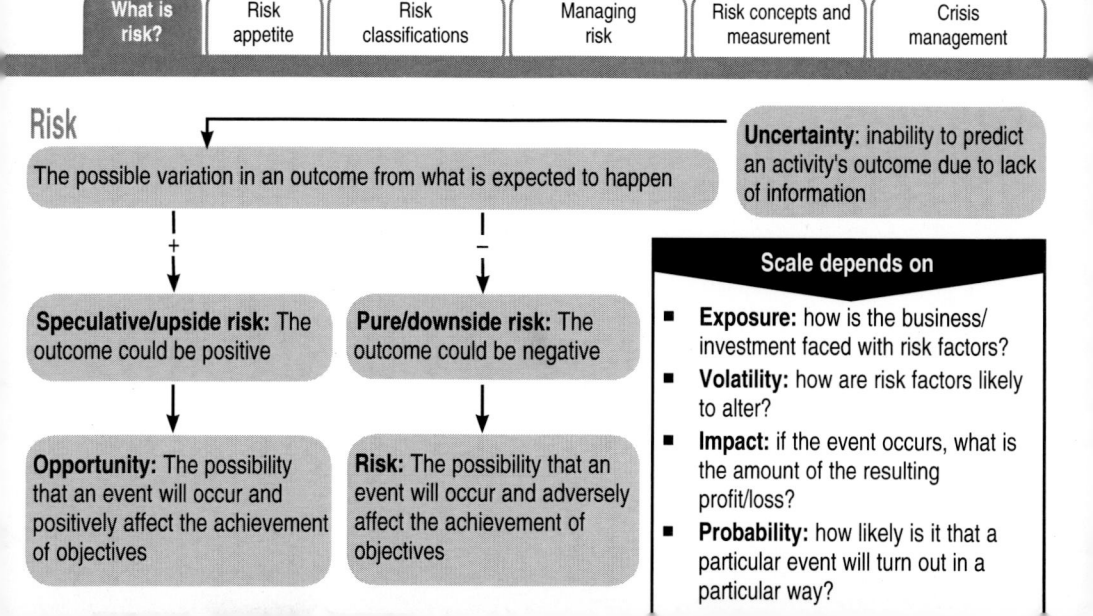

Risk

Risk

The possible variation in an outcome from what is expected to happen

Uncertainty: inability to predict an activity's outcome due to lack of information

+

−

Speculative/upside risk: The outcome could be positive

Pure/downside risk: The outcome could be negative

Opportunity: The possibility that an event will occur and positively affect the achievement of objectives

Risk: The possibility that an event will occur and adversely affect the achievement of objectives

Scale depends on

- **Exposure:** how is the business/investment faced with risk factors?
- **Volatility:** how are risk factors likely to alter?
- **Impact:** if the event occurs, what is the amount of the resulting profit/loss?
- **Probability:** how likely is it that a particular event will turn out in a particular way?

Management set objectives

Identify/assess risks to achievement of objectives

Risk appetite is the extent to which the business is prepared to take on risks in order to achieve objectives

Risk averse   Risk neutral   Risk seeking

Select least risky investment   Select investment with highest **expected returns**   Select highest risk investment

Expected return = weighted average of possible returns × probability of each occurring

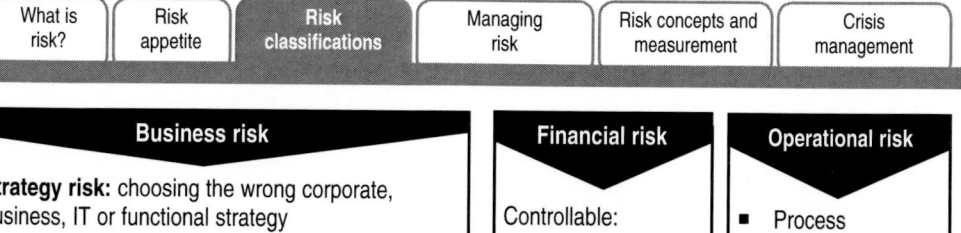

Business risk

- **Strategy risk:** choosing the wrong corporate, business, IT or functional strategy
- **Enterprise risk:** a project fails because it should not have been taken on
- **Product risk:** product/services will not appeal to customers

Financial risk

Controllable:

- Liquidity
- Gearing
- Credit

Uncontrollable:

- Foreign exchange
- Interest rate
- Market

Operational risk

- Process
- People
- Systems
- Event

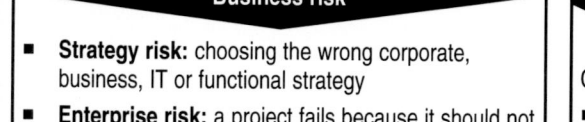

Cyber risk

- Phishing
- Webcam manager
- File hijacker
- Keylogging
- Screenshot manager
- Ad clicker
- Hacking
- DDos attack

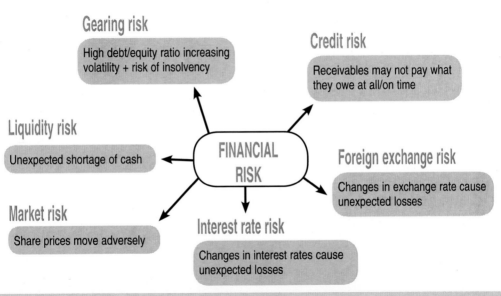

Gearing risk

High debt/equity ratio increasing
volatility + risk of insolvency

Credit risk

Receivables may not pay what
they owe at all/on time

Liquidity risk

Unexpected shortage of cash

FINANCIAL
RISK

Foreign exchange risk

Changes in exchange rate cause
unexpected losses

Market risk

Share prices move adversely

Interest rate risk

Changes in interest rates cause
unexpected losses

5: Introduction to risk management

OPERATIONAL RISK

Disaster risk
Risk of loss due to single, unlikely event, which may have serious consequences

People risk
Risks from staff constraints, incompetence, dishonesty

Process risk
Organisation's processes may be ineffective/inefficient

Regulatory risk
New regulations affect operations

Event risk
Risk of loss due to single event

Systems risk
Risks arising from information and communications systems

Reputation risk
Business activities damage its reputation in stakeholders' eyes

Systemic risk
Failure in business's systems or supply chain

Legal risk
Risk of loss from contract that cannot legally be enforced

Disaster risk

Risks

- **Fire**
  - Site preparation eg, fire proof materials
  - Detection eg, smoke detectors
  - Extinguishers eg, sprinklers
- **Water**
  - Waterproof ceilings
  - Adequate drainage
- **Other measures**
  - Physical access controls
  - Good office layout
  - Protected power supplies
  - Separate generator

Disaster recovery plan

- **Responsibilities** including overall manager and subordinates
- **Priorities** – establish most important tasks needing computer time
- **Backup/standby** – with other company/manual processing
- **Communication** – tell staff details/implications/actions
- **Public relations** – managing external concerns
- **Risk assessment** – risk of recurrence of problem/occurrence elsewhere in organisation

Risk management

Identification, analysis and economic control of risks which threaten the business's assets or earning capacity

- Minimise exposure
- Reduce probability
- Limit impact
- Many businesses focus on risks to CSFs during strategic planning

Formal risk management requirements

- The law (such as, car insurance)

- Regulatory bodies (ICAEW requires PII; UK Corporate Governance Code requires risk-based management approach to corporate governance)

- Contract (such as mortgages require buildings insurance)

Managing cyber risk

- Understand the impact of cyber attack
- Implement basic cyber security
- Take cyber security further with 10 Steps to Cyber Security or an international standard and an enterprise cyber security mindset
- Apply cyber security to all areas of your business
- Maintain and share awareness of current threats

Risk management process

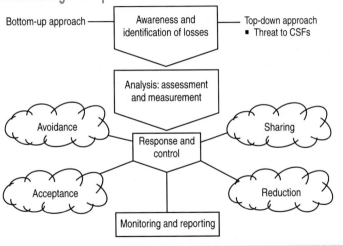

Bottom-up approach — **Awareness and identification of losses**

Top-down approach
- Threat to CSFs

Analysis: assessment and measurement

Avoidance

Sharing

Response and control

Acceptance

Reduction

Monitoring and reporting

Types of significant loss

- Property
- Liability to third parties
- Personnel
- Pecuniary loss regarding receivables
- Interruption

Risk assessment

Consider the nature of each risk, its implications and its potential seriousness

Risk measurement

Identify the probability of the risk occurring and quantify the resultant impact

Risk response and control

- **Risk avoidance** – Not investing in high risk/high cost operations
- **Risk reduction** – Contingency planning, physical measures (alarms, fire precautions) awareness and commitment
- **Risk acceptance/retention** – Bear full cost if risk materialises; valid if risks insignificant or avoidance costs too great
- **Risk transfer/sharing** – to suppliers, customers, insurers, state; with insurers/joint venture partners

Probability × Impact = **Expected value** of **gross risk** (uncontrolled)

Risk monitoring and reporting

Monitoring should be ongoing and continuous; action should be taken promptly as a result (= control):

- Corrective action on risk
- Review of identification and response processes

Risk management issues must be reported to the appropriate persons in management hierarchy

Analysis of risk may involve use of statistics

Measures of central tendency

Median = middle value in a set of data

Mode = most frequently occurring item

Mean = $\overline{X} = \Sigma(x)/n$

Expected return = weighted average of possible outcomes (weighted according to probability)

Measures of dispersion (spread)

Range = highest value - lowest value

Deviation - how far a value is from mean

Variance = average of square deviations from mean

Standard deviation = square root of variance

Coefficient of variation = $\dfrac{Standard\ deviation}{mean}$

Evaluation of measures

	Mean	Median	Mode
Advantages	■ Widely understood (average) ■ Representative of all values in data ■ Can be used in further statistical analysis	■ Easy to understand ■ Not distorted by outliers	■ Easy to find and understand ■ Will always take a value equal to an actual value in the data ■ Can be used for qualitative data ■ Not distorted by outliers
Disadvantages	■ Value may not be the same as any actual values in the data ■ May return same value for very different sets of data ■ May be distorted by outliers	■ Value may not be the same as any actual values in the data ■ Calculation of it does not use all data in data set therefore not representative ■ Difficult to identify in large data sets ■ Not suited to further statistical analysis	■ Calculation of it does not use all data in data set therefore not representative ■ Not suited to further statistical analysis

Normal distribution

Many large data sets approximate a normal distribution:

Where:

μ = mean = median = mode

σ = standard deviation

Area under curve shows probability of ranges of values occurring (eg, 34.1% of values lie between the mean and one standard deviation above the mean).

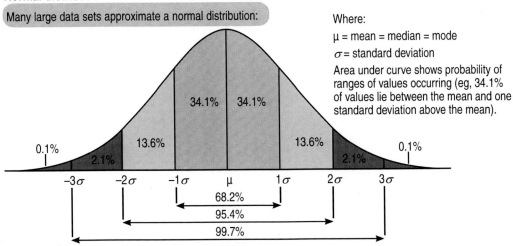

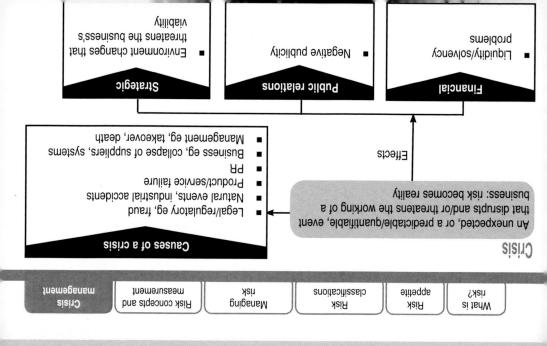

Crisis

An unexpected, or a predictable/quantifiable, event that disrupts and/or threatens the working of a business: risk becomes reality

Causes of a crisis

- Legal/regulatory eg, fraud
- Natural events, industrial accidents
- Product/service failure
- PR
- Business eg, collapse of suppliers, systems
- Management eg, takeover, death

Effects

Financial
- Liquidity/solvency problems

Public relations
- Negative publicity

Strategic
- Environment changes that threatens the business's viability

The business's crisis management process should:

1 **Prevent** a crisis from occurring = crisis prevention

2 **Plan** for what to do in the event of a crisis occurring = contingency planning

Crisis management

Identifying a crisis, planning a response, confronting the crisis and resolving it.

1 Assess the cause and its short and long-term effects

2 Project the most likely course of the crisis

3 Focus resources on solving the crisis

4 Look for opportunities

Business resilience

Business resilience is the ability of a business to manage and survive against planned or unplanned shocks and disruptions to its operations.

Features of resilient organisations

- Diversified resources and assets to facilitate alternative approaches and adaptation to change
- Strong relationships and networks (both internal and external)
- The ability to respond rapidly and decisively to an emerging crisis
- They review and adapt based on experience and changing circumstances

Challenges to building a resilient organisation

- Lack of expertise
- Lack of input from senior management
- Siloes for delivery
- Limited sharing of risk information

The following **four metrics measure resilience:**

Metric	Description
Compliance	How well the organisation complies with its standards and policies
Completeness	The scope of resilience (ie, how wide a range of issues is the organisation prepared for)
Value	Qualitative and quantitative measures of how well the organisation can meet specific outcomes
Capability	Evidence, collected through exercises and reviews, of the extent to which the organisation has put resilience processes and procedures in place

Business continuity plans

A **business continuity plan** will typically provide for:

- **Standby procedures** so that some operations can be performed while normal services are disrupted
- **Recovery procedures** once the cause of the breakdown has been discovered or corrected
- **Personnel management** policies to ensure that the above are implemented properly

The plan must cover all activities from the **initial response** to the disaster (crisis management), through to **damage limitation** and **full recovery**. Responsibilities must be clearly spelt out for all tasks.

> **Contents of a business continuity plan**
> - Definition of responsibilities
> - Priorities
> - Backup and standby arrangements
> - Communication with staff
> - Public relations
> - Risk assessment

| What is risk? | Risk appetite | Risk classifications | Managing risk | Risk concepts and measurement | Crisis management |

6: The finance function and financial information

Topic List

Financial information

Uses of financial information

Financial statements

The finance function

Measuring performance

Financial control processes

Internal controls

The production of financial information lies at the heart of accountancy. In this chapter we look at types of financial information and their uses, at information systems and security, and at the uses of financial statements.

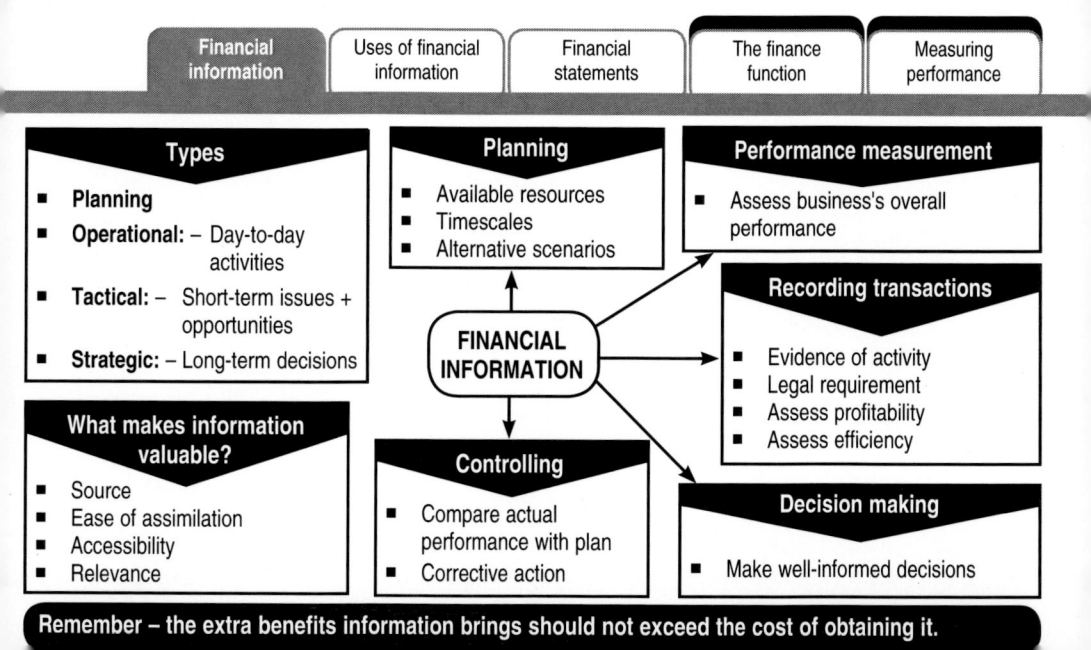

1 To help make economic decisions:

Interested users

- Buy, hold or sell shares? → Present/potential investors
- Receive benefits from employer? → Employees/directors
- Lending and interest payment? → Lenders
- Source of supply secure? → Customers
- Receive payment → Suppliers
- Allocate resources, regulate securities, receive tax income? → Government + its agencies
- Contribution to local economy → The public

2 To help make managers accountable for their stewardship of business's resources → All

To make **economic decisions** users need to evaluate the **ability** of the business to generate cash, and the **timing** and **certainty** of cash flows. Therefore they need information contained in **financial statements**

1 Financial position = statement of financial position

Relevant factors

- Economic resources controlled
- Financial structure
- Liquidity
- Solvency
- Adaptability

Information needed to predict

- Ability to generate cash in future
- Borrowing, distribution of profit, new equity
- Availability of positive net cash in near future
- Availability of positive net cash in longer term
- Capacity to adapt to environment changes

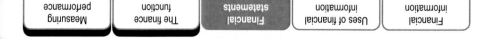

2 **Financial performance = statement of profit or loss and other comprehensive income**

Information on variability in profitability

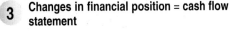

Needed to predict
■ Changes in economic resources
■ Capacity to generate cash from existing resources
■ How well it might use new resources

3 **Changes in financial position = cash flow statement**

Information on past cash flows

Needed to assess
■ How able it is at generating cash
■ How well it uses generated cash

| Financial information | Uses of financial information | **Financial statements** | The finance function | Measuring performance |

Qualitative characteristics

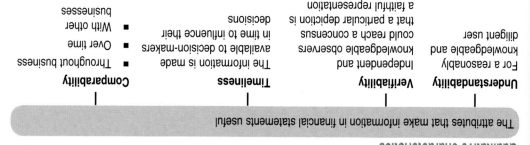

The attributes that make information in financial statements useful

Understandability

For a reasonably knowledgeable and diligent user

Verifiability

Independent and knowledgeable observers could reach a concensus that a particular depiction is a faithful representation

Timeliness

The information is made available to decision-makers in time to influence their decisions

Comparability

- Throughout business
- Over time
- With other businesses

Limitations in meeting users' needs

1 **Presentation**

- Highly standardised
- Highly aggregated

2 **Backward-looking**

- Historical focus, not on future

3 **Omission of non-financial information**

- Narrative descriptions
- Risks and opportunities
- Analysis of performance and prospects
- Governance

Effects of poor financial information

- Fails to meet users' needs
- Is not understandable, relevant, reliable or comparable

so

- **Integrity of financial markets** is undermined
- **Public interest** is not served

Usually covered in Chairman's Statement and Directors' Report

Tasks of finance function

1 **Recording financial transactions and controlling resources**

2 **Management accounting for internal users**

- Internal reporting for management and control
- Cost accounting
- Forecasting and budgets
- Assist with decision making
- Measuring performance
- Analysing investment decisions
- Pricing

3 **Treasury management**

- Preparing cash budgets
- Managing surpluses/deficits of cash, and investment
- Managing inventory, receivables and payables to optimise cash flow
- Analysing financing decisions
- Managing foreign exchange
- Managing financial risk
- Raising long-term debt/equity finance

4 **Financial reporting to external users**

- Financial statements
- Tax
- Regulatory

Purpose of finance function

To support pursuit of business objectives by:

- Undertaking **transaction processing** and ensuring there are sufficient **financial control processes**
- Providing information to **support decisions** and **measure performance**, **performance measurement**
- Ensuring there is sufficient **liquidity and solvency**
- Acting as **sources of financial expertise** through **business partnering** to provide insights into the performance of the business functions that they are embedded in.

Measuring performance

1 Identify need for performance measurement

2 Identify relevant information

3 Calculate performance measures – absolute or relative

4 Compare the measure with
- Trends over time
- Budgets, targets and standards
- Results of other SBUs
- Results of other businesses
- The economy in general

5 Take action as required

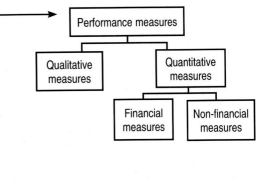

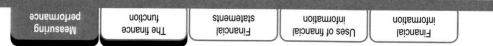

Financial information | Uses of financial information | Financial statements | The finance function | Measuring performance

How to measure achievement of objectives

- Profitability
- Liquidity/solvency
- Activity levels
- Productivity
- Effectiveness
- Efficiency
- Investor appeal

So that

- Managers can make control decisions
- Directors can assess corporate governance
- External users can make economic decisions

Limitations of performance measures

- Identifying trends + making comparisons
- Timelines and appropriate use of data

Financial measures

- Working capital ratios
- Cash flow
- EPS
- Share price
- Variance analysis
- Revenue targets
- Market share targets
- Customer profitability analysis
- Profit and margins
- ROI and RI
- Labour rates

- Calculate variance of actual from budget/standard
- Volume
- Prices/rates
- Usage
- Efficiency

Non-financial measures

- Customer returns
- Enquiries
- Customer satisfaction
- Late deliveries
- Quality
- Labour turnover
- Labour skills
- Production performance
- Innovation

Note: A combination of the two types is best.

The balanced scorecard

Customer perspective

'How do customers see us?' This perspective concentrates on customers' concern with time, quality, performance and service. Example measures would be percentage of on-time deliveries and customer rejection rates.

Innovation and learning perspective

'Can we continue to improve and create value?' This perspective is forward looking and concentrates on what the company must do to satisfy future needs. Performance measures include time-to-market for new products and percentage of revenue from them.

Internal business perspective

'What must we excel at?' This perspective focuses on what the company must be internally to meet its customers' expectations. Control measures will focus on, for example, core competence, skills, productivity and cost.

Financial perspective

'How do we appear to shareholders?' This is the traditional reporting perspective, but includes ROI, RI and EVA®. Market share and sales growth are included here.

| Financial information | Uses of financial information | Financial statements | The finance function | Measuring performance |

Sustainability, natural capital and climate change

Sustainability

Global Reporting Initiative standards propose contents of sustainability reports showing organisation's direct and indirect impacts on sustainability under three headings:

- Economic
- Environmental
- Social

Natural capital

Climate Disclosure Standards Board provides a framework to ensure information about natural capital is given same prominence as financial capital in mainstream reports. Uses qualitative characteristics that are consistent with IFRS.

Climate change

FRC requires boards of UK companies to consider impact of business decisions on climate change.

UN Task Force on climate-related Financial Disclosures requires greater disclosure of climate related issues under four headings:

- Governance
- Strategy
- Risk management
- Metrics and targets

The finance function must establish adequate **financial control processes**, a form of internal control, in the business.

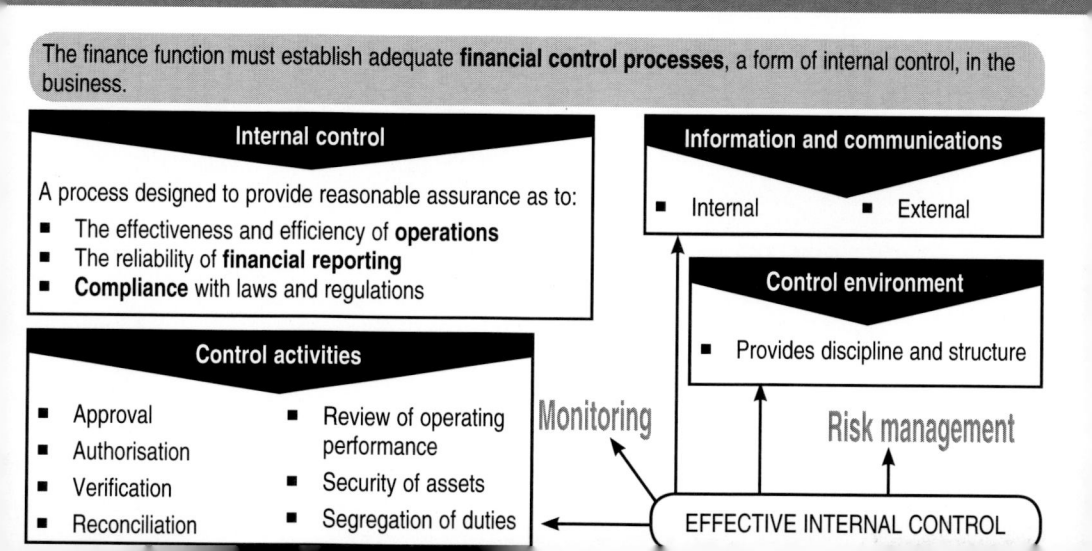

Internal control

A process designed to provide reasonable assurance as to:

- The effectiveness and efficiency of **operations**
- The reliability of **financial reporting**
- **Compliance** with laws and regulations

Information and communications

- Internal
- External

Control environment

- Provides discipline and structure

Control activities

- Approval
- Authorisation
- Verification
- Reconciliation
- Review of operating performance
- Security of assets
- Segregation of duties

Monitoring

Risk management

EFFECTIVE INTERNAL CONTROL

Internal control

A process designed to provide reasonable assurance regarding the achievement of objectives via:

- Effective and efficient operations
- Reliable financial reporting
- Compliance with laws/regulations

Sound system of internal control does **not** eliminate risk of:

- Poor judgement in decision making
- Human error
- Deliberate circumvention of control processes
- Management override
- Unforeseen circumstances occurring

Notes

7: Business finance

Topic List

Risk v return

The banking system and money markets

Sources of finance

Businesses require finance in order to achieve their objectives. The sources and methods of finance, and their relationship with risk and return, are covered in this chapter.

Risk vs return

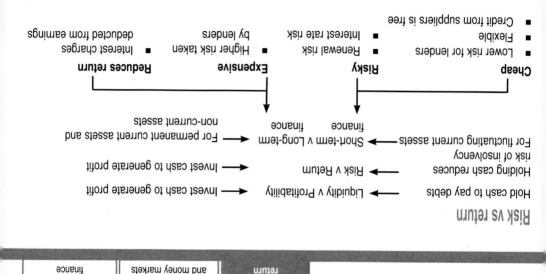

Hold cash to pay debts → **Liquidity v Profitability** → Invest cash to generate profit

Holding cash reduces risk of insolvency → **Risk v Return** → Invest cash to generate profit

For fluctuating current assets → **Short-term v Long-term finance** → For permanent current assets and non-current assets

Cheap	Risky	Expensive	Reduces return
■ Lower risk for lenders	■ Renewal risk	■ Higher risk taken by lenders	■ Interest charges deducted from earnings
■ Flexible	■ Interest rate risk		
■ Credit from suppliers is free			

The banking system

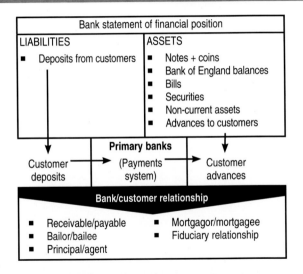

Bank's duties

- Honour customer's cheques
- Credit funds to customer's account
- Repay funds on demand
- Comply with customer's instructions
- Provide statements
- Respect confidentiality

Bank's rights

- Reasonable charges
- Use funds
- Receive repayment of overdraft on demand
- Indemnity from customer

Customer's duties

- Exercise care
- Tell bank of known forgeries

Capital markets

- **London Stock Exchange:**

    1 **Main market**, with firm regulation, for raising funds through new issues of shares (primary market), and trading existing shares (secondary market)

    2 **AIM (Alternative Investment Market):** for newer companies, less firmly regulated

    3 **Professional Securities Market (PSM):** allows businesses to raise capital from professional investors

- **Gilt edged market** for UK government stock

- **International capital markets** are operated between banks in larger countries to provide major finance for very large companies and institutions. Confusingly, their securities are known as eurobonds

- Certain stocks not traded on recognised stock exchanges are traded in **over the counter** markets

Money markets

Short-term investment and borrowing of funds is handled in the **money markets**. These are operated by the banks and other financial institutions and include markets for:

- Certificates of deposit
- Bills of exchange and commercial paper
- Treasury bills
- Building society bulk borrowing
- Local authority bills and other short-term borrowing

Sources of finance

Equity		Debt	
■ Retained earnings		■ Overdraft	
■ Rights issues		■ Factoring	
■ New issues		■ Term loans	
■ Preference shares		■ Loan stock	
		■ Leasing	

Business angels

Wealthy individuals who invest in new or expanding businesses, often collectively

Venture capital

The provision of risk-bearing capital, usually in the form of a participation in equity, to companies with high growth potential

Green finance

Any financial instrument used to raise finance for projects that deliver positive environmental benefits

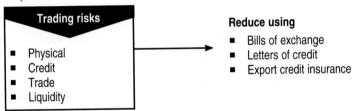

Exports

Trading risks

- Physical
- Credit
- Trade
- Liquidity

Reduce using

- Bills of exchange
- Letters of credit
- Export credit insurance

Notes

8: The professional accountant

Topic List

The accountancy profession

The professional accountant

Accounting standards

Regulation of the profession

ICAEW

FRC

In this chapter we look at the purpose, importance and work of the accountancy profession, at the requirements for technical competence and professional responsibility from professional accountants, at the roles accountants play in society and at the purpose and uses of accounting principles and standards.

We also examine the regulation of the accountancy profession.

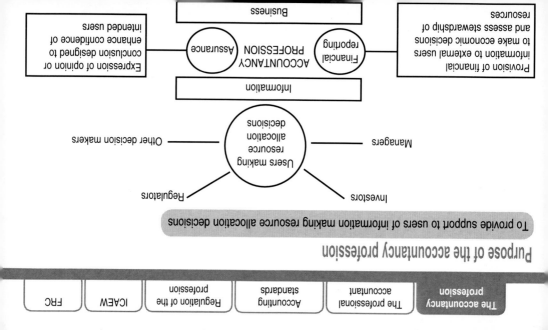

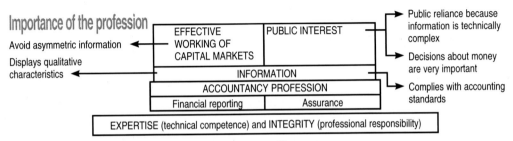

Importance of the profession

Avoid asymmetric information ←

Displays qualitative characteristics ←

EFFECTIVE WORKING OF CAPITAL MARKETS | **PUBLIC INTEREST**

INFORMATION

ACCOUNTANCY PROFESSION

Financial reporting | Assurance

→ Public reliance because information is technically complex

→ Decisions about money are very important

→ Complies with accounting standards

EXPERTISE (technical competence) and INTEGRITY (professional responsibility)

Work of the professional accountant

1 Maintaining control and safeguarding assets

- Complete, timely, accurate, transactions recording
- Sufficient internal controls
- Properly constituted + informed audit committee
- Qualified and resourced non-executive directors

2 Financial management

Raising and using financial resources

- New finance
- Using funds to achieve objectives
- Planning control
- Treasury management
- Risk management

3 Financial reporting

- Apply professional principles
- Apply accounting principles

The accountancy profession	**The professional accountant**	Accounting standards	Regulation of the profession	ICAEW	FRC

Technical competence

The professional accountant requires **technical competence** and **professional responsibility**.

This is assured by:

1 Entry and education requirements of ICAEW

- ≥ Two A levels plus 3 GCSEs
- 450 day training contract
- Course of theoretical instruction
- PASS ICAEW exams
- Certificate of suitability
- Pay admission + subscription fees

→
- Knowledge and understanding
- Skills and abilities
- Personal commitment and professional principles
- Professional scepticism

2 Requirements for continuing membership of ICAEW

FOR ALL MEMBERS
- Obey rules + regulations
- Pay annual subscription fee
- Undertake Continuing Professional Education (CPE)

FOR MEMBERS IN PUBLIC PRACTICE
- Practising certificate

Plus:
- Implement Code of Ethics
- Have professional indemnity insurance (PII)

3 Requirement for ICAEW members in reserved areas

- Statutory audit
- Investment business
- Insolvency
- Probate

Comply with regulations set by ICAEW or recognised professional regulator on eligibility, conduct and competence

Roles of the professional accountant

In practice		In business
RESERVED AREAS	**NON-RESERVED AREAS**	<ul><li>Wide number of business areas</li><li>Wide number of roles</li><li>Roles/responsibilities limited by requirement to act with professional competence and due care</li></ul>
<ul><li>Investment business</li><li>Insolvency</li><li>Audit</li><li>Probate</li></ul>	<ul><li>Accounting</li><li>Tax</li><li>Management consulting</li><li>Financial management</li><li>Corporate finance</li><li>ICT</li><li>Forensic accounting</li></ul>	

Must be:

- Member of recognised supervisory body eg, ICAEW
- Appropriately qualified

May be:

- Sole practitioner, partnership or LLP

May NOT be:

- Officer/employee of company
- Partner/employee of such a person

Purpose of accounting standards

> To identify proper accounting practice for preparers, auditors + users of financial statements

Types of accounting standards

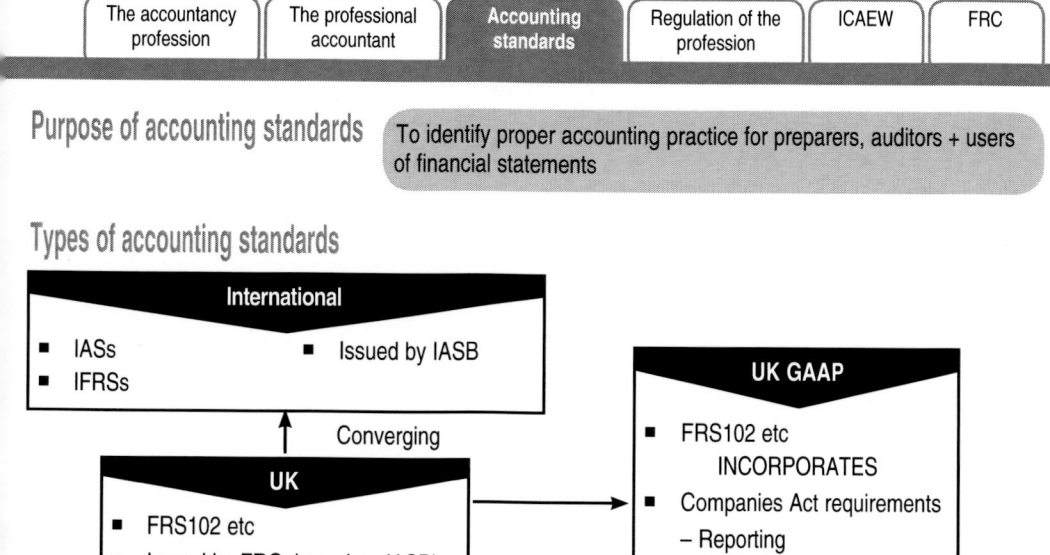

International

- IASs
- IFRSs
- Issued by IASB

Converging

UK

- FRS102 etc
- Issued by FRC, based on IASB's IFRS for SMEs

UK GAAP

- FRS102 etc
  INCORPORATES
- Companies Act requirements
  - Reporting
  - Accounting records
  - Statutory audit

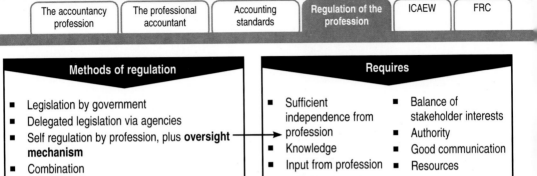

Methods of regulation

- Legislation by government
- Delegated legislation via agencies
- Self regulation by profession, plus **oversight mechanism**
- Combination

Requires

- Sufficient independence from profession
- Knowledge
- Input from profession
- Balance of stakeholder interests
- Authority
- Good communication
- Resources

Aims of oversight mechanism

- **Protect public interest** from:
  - Being misled
  - Abuse of power through asymmetric information/monopoly
- Facilitate competition/reduce trade barriers
- Ensure high technical, ethical and educational standards
- Flexibility
- Transparency; 'justice is seen to be done'
- Fairness

ICAEW has primary responsibility for supervising ICAEW members in their professional capacity.

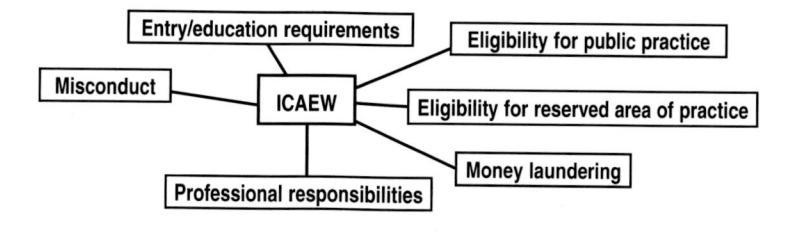

Structure of the Financial Reporting Council (FRC)

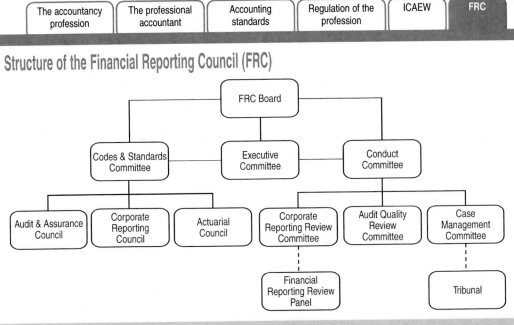

Notes

9: Governance and ethics

Topic List

Why is governance an issue?

Good corporate governance

Governance structures

Ethics-based culture

Natural capital, sustainability and corporate responsibility

In this chapter we look at the ideas underlying corporate governance and its structures, and at ethical culture and business values.

Governance

The system by which businesses are directed and controlled

Agency theory

Proposes that, whilst individual team members act in their own self-interest, individual well-being depends on the well-being of other individuals and on the performance of the team

Businesses are set of contracts between principals (suppliers of finance) and agents (directors).

The agency problem

If directors don't have significant shareholdings, they can under-perform and over-reward themselves because:

- They have better information
- They are insufficiently accountable

Stewardship perspective

Directors have company's best interest at heart; they are the stewards of the asset so shareholders take little or no part in running it

Public policy perspective

As corporate perspective, plus interests of public at large

As reflected in South Africa's King Report (its core aspects are leadership, sustainability and good corporate citizenship).

Corporate perspective

Directors balance shareholder and other linked stakeholder interests to maximise company wealth

Stakeholder perspective

Directors have a duty of care to the wider community of stakeholders

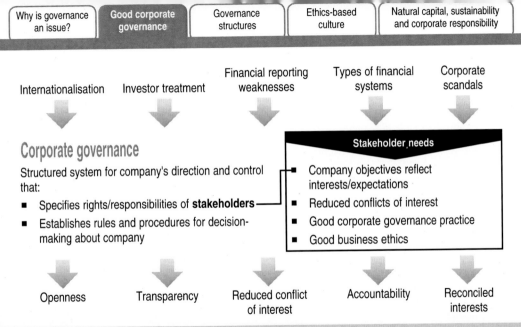

Internationalisation   Investor treatment   Financial reporting weaknesses   Types of financial systems   Corporate scandals

Corporate governance

Structured system for company's direction and control that:

- Specifies rights/responsibilities of **stakeholders**
- Establishes rules and procedures for decision-making about company

Stakeholder needs

- Company objectives reflect interests/expectations
- Reduced conflicts of interest
- Good corporate governance practice
- Good business ethics

Openness   Transparency   Reduced conflict of interest   Accountability   Reconciled interests

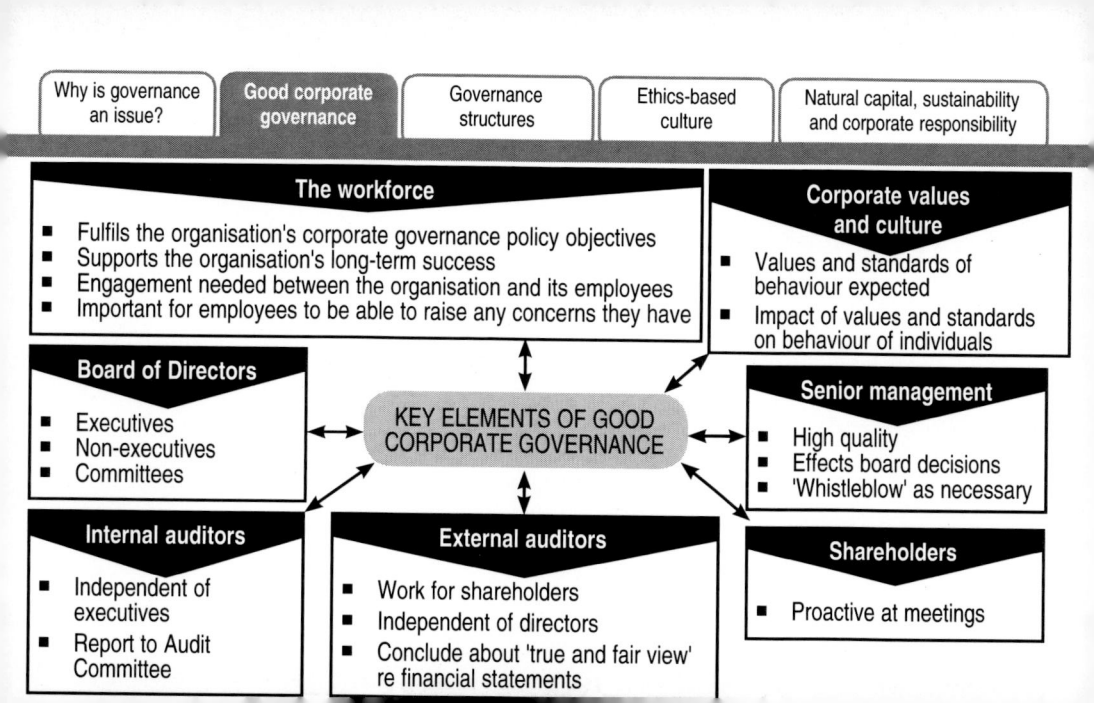

The workforce

- Fulfils the organisation's corporate governance policy objectives
- Supports the organisation's long-term success
- Engagement needed between the organisation and its employees
- Important for employees to be able to raise any concerns they have

Corporate values and culture

- Values and standards of behaviour expected
- Impact of values and standards on behaviour of individuals

Board of Directors

- Executives
- Non-executives
- Committees

KEY ELEMENTS OF GOOD CORPORATE GOVERNANCE

Senior management

- High quality
- Effects board decisions
- 'Whistleblow' as necessary

Internal auditors

- Independent of executives
- Report to Audit Committee

External auditors

- Work for shareholders
- Independent of directors
- Conclude about 'true and fair view' re financial statements

Shareholders

- Proactive at meetings

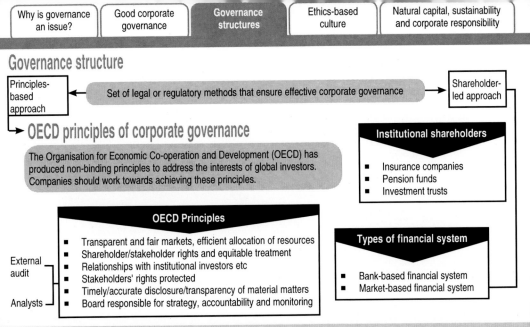

Governance structure

Principles-based approach ← Set of legal or regulatory methods that ensure effective corporate governance → Shareholder-led approach

→ OECD principles of corporate governance

The Organisation for Economic Co-operation and Development (OECD) has produced non-binding principles to address the interests of global investors. Companies should work towards achieving these principles.

Institutional shareholders

- Insurance companies
- Pension funds
- Investment trusts

OECD Principles

External audit —

- Transparent and fair markets, efficient allocation of resources
- Shareholder/stakeholder rights and equitable treatment
- Relationships with institutional investors etc
- Stakeholders' rights protected
- Timely/accurate disclosure/transparency of material matters

Analysts —

- Board responsible for strategy, accountability and monitoring

Types of financial system

- Bank-based financial system
- Market-based financial system

9: Governance and ethics

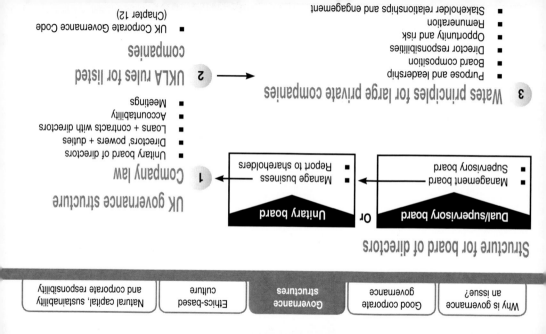

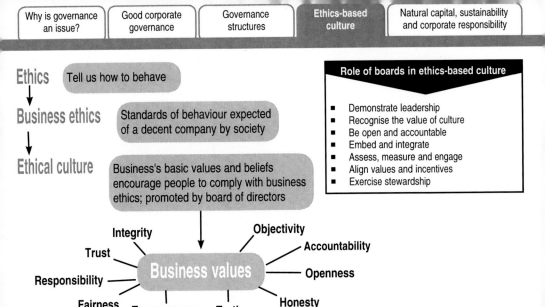

Ethics — Tell us how to behave

Business ethics — Standards of behaviour expected of a decent company by society

Ethical culture — Business's basic values and beliefs encourage people to comply with business ethics; promoted by board of directors

Role of boards in ethics-based culture

- Demonstrate leadership
- Recognise the value of culture
- Be open and accountable
- Embed and integrate
- Assess, measure and engage
- Align values and incentives
- Exercise stewardship

Business values

- Integrity
- Objectivity
- Accountability
- Trust
- Openness
- Responsibility
- Honesty
- Fairness
- Transparency
- Truth

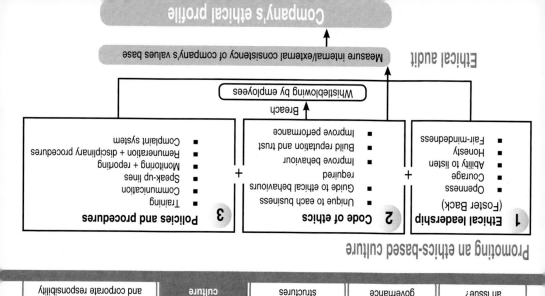

Why promote an ethics-based culture?

- Meet legal requirements
- Build trust and credibility
- Gain external verification and certification
- Gain or restore stakeholder confidence
- Improve management systems through standards and processes

How ethics affects different business functions

Business function	Impact on ethics
Marketing	**Targeting of marketing efforts** Is it ethical to target children or vulnerable people?
Operations	**Production processes** Should the organisation use the cheapest method of production, rather than more expensive, but more environmentally friendly alternatives?
Procurement	**Sourcing of materials** Is it ethical to source meat and animal products from cheap suppliers with low standards of animal welfare? Should the organisation use overseas suppliers that exploit workers with poor pay and conditions, or which pollute their local environments?
HR	**Terms of employee contracts** Are zero hours contracts and low pay rates ethical?

Business function	Impact on ethics
IT	**Privacy and security of data** As well as a legal obligation, organisations have an ethical obligation to collect, store and manage data in a way that is in the best interests of those that the data concerns
Finance	**Paying suppliers** Should large organisations take advantage of small suppliers by forcing down prices, or by demanding long credit periods, as a way of improving their cash operating cycle? **Tax strategy** Should multinational companies structure their business so that profits are taxed in countries with low tax rates? Minimising tax costs will help to maximise the value a company can deliver to its shareholders, but is it 'fair' to deprive governments of tax revenue which could help fund public services such as healthcare and education?

Natural capital: 'the world's stocks of natural assets which include geology, soil, air, water and all living things.' World Forum On Natural Capital (n.d.)

Sustainability: ability to 'meet the needs of the present without compromising the ability of future generations to meet their own needs'

Business sustainability: how far a business operates in a sustainable way, interacting with individuals and governments.

↓

Corporate responsibility: the commitment the business makes to its stakeholders to increase its positive impacts and decrease its negative ones. (Institute of Business Ethics).

10: Corporate governance

Topic List

The UK Corporate Governance Code

Role of audit

In this chapter we look at the details of the UK Corporate Governance Code, issued by the FRC as a voluntary code of practice. However, for premium listed UK companies, these are effectively compulsory.

The UK Corporate Governance Code is set out in the form of **principles**, with supporting provisions.

Role of the board

Every company should be headed by an effective board, which is collectively responsible for the long-term success of the company

- Board gives entrepreneurial leadership
- Board sets strategic aims, plus values and standards
- Board ensures necessary resources are in place for the company to meet its objectives
- Board reviews management performance

Chairman and Chief Executive

There should be a clear division of responsibilities at the head of the company between running the company (the Chairman) and running the board (the Chief Executive)

- Chief Executive and Chairman should be different people
- Chief Executive should not go on to be Chairman on retirement

Board composition

The board should have the appropriate **balance** of **skills**, **experience**, **independence** and **knowledge** of the company

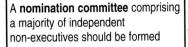

- At least half the board, excluding the chair should be **independent** non-executives
- The board should be the right size
- Membership of board committees should be refreshed regularly

Board appointment

A **nomination committee** comprising a majority of independent non-executives should be formed

There should be a formal, rigorous and transparent procedure for appointment to the board

Information and resources

The board, supported by the company secretary, should ensure that it has the policies, processes, information, time and resources it needs to function effectively and efficiently

Evaluating performance

The board should undertake formal and rigorous annual evaluations of its performance and that of its committees and individual directors.

- Individual directors to be evaluated
- Chairman to act on identified strengths and weaknesses, handling proposing new members/rejection of weak members

Re-election of directors

The re-election of directors should be subject to continued satisfactory performance.

- All directors should be subject to annual re-election
- The annual report should describe the work of the nomination committee

Directors' remuneration

Executive directors' remuneration should promote the long-term success of the company. Performance-related elements should be transparent, stretching and rigorously applied.

- **Remuneration committee** to monitor levels of remuneration, service contracts and compensation payments
- Remuneration policy should cover performance related elements, executive share options, and non-executive pay

Transparency of remuneration

There should be a formal and transparent procedure for developing policy on executive remuneration, and remuneration packages of individual directors. No director should be involved in deciding his/her own remuneration.

- Remuneration committee to be comprised of independent non-executives

Financial reporting

The board should present a balanced and understandable assessment of the company's position and prospects.

- Directors must state their responsibility for financial statements in the annual report, whether the going concern basis of accounting has been adopted and any material uncertainties about the going concern status over the next 12 months

- Annual robust assessment of the principal risks facing the company, including those that would threaten its business model, future performance, solvency or liquidity

- State they expect the company to continue in operation and meet its liabilities as they fall due

Risk management and internal control

The board should determine the nature and extent of the principal risks it is willing to take in achieving its strategic objectives, and maintain sound risk management and internal control.

- Annual review by board of risk management and internal control systems

Auditing

The board should establish formal and transparent arrangements for considering how they should apply corporate reporting, risk management and internal control principles.

Audit committee consisting of independent non-executives, at least one with recent and relevant financial experience. The audit committee as a whole shall have competence relevant to the sector in which the company operates.

Risk management and internal control

Responsibility of board of directors for sound system of risk management and internal control

- Robust assessment of principal risks facing the company and of its prospects
- Policy-making for financial, operational and compliance controls
- Review system's effectiveness in addressing identified risks
- Annual report on internal control system to shareholders

Statement on internal control

- Acknowledge responsibility
- Manage not eliminate risk
- Reasonable, not absolute assurance
- Ongoing process
- Regular review of systems
- Compliance with FRC guidance
- A reasonable expectation that the company will be able to continue in operation and meet its liabilities

External audit

Purpose: To issue an opinion in an audit report as to whether the financial statements give a true and fair view of the company's financial performance for the period, and of its financial position at the year-end

Additional reports:
- On the director's remuneration report
- On compliance with the UK Corporate Governance Code

Appointment:
- Recommended by audit committee and board
- Voted on by shareholders

Prevention/detection of fraud and error: NOT responsibility of external auditor

Directors

Must satisfy themselves that the internal control and risk management systems operate effectively

→

Managers

Must implement and monitor these → Internal audit

Internal audit (IA)

Monitors effective operation of internal control and risk management systems

Areas covered by IA

- Operational controls
- Financial controls
- Compliance (financial and non-financial)

Role of Audit Committee

- Appoints head of IA
- Ensures sufficient resources are available for IA

Tasks of IA

Assess:
- Risk identification, analysis and management

Advise on:
- Embedding risk management processes
- Improving internal controls

Ensure:
- Safeguarding of assets
- Effective and efficient operations
- Compliance with laws/regulations
- Reliable/accurate records and reports

Help with:
- Detection of error/fraud
- Identifying savings/opportunities

Notes

11: The economic environment of business and finance

The economic environment of a business is determined by the forces of supply and demand, and by government regulation.

Economics

The production and consumption of goods and services: what to produce, how to produce it and who to produce it for

Market economy		Mixed economy		Command economy
Free markets and private ownership	—	Market system with some regulation	—	Government planning and control

The production of goods and services requires the utilisation of economic **resources** or **factors of production**.

These resources are **scarce** and therefore choices must be made as to how they are to be employed.

- **LAND** includes all **natural resources**. Land itself is limited in quantity but can be improved in quality.
- **LABOUR** is people employed to produce goods and services. It varies in quality.
- **CAPITAL** consists of physical goods that aid production. Money can be transformed into capital.
- **ENTERPRISE** is needed both to organise production and to take the risk of possible financial loss.

A market

Potential buyers and potential sellers come together for the purpose of exchange

Market structure

The number of buyers and sellers in a market and their relative bargaining power

The firm

Sellers are **firms**; buyers of consumer goods and services are **households**

Microeconomic environment

How the market mechanism of the interaction of supply and demand for an item affects a particular firm

Macroeconomic environment

The world in which all firms operate, incorporating global and national influences

Role of government in the national economy

- **Producer**, of certain goods and services
- **Purchaser**, of final goods and services
- **Investment**, in roads, schools, hospitals etc
- **Transfer payments**, between one section of the economy and another

Factors affecting consumption in an economy

- Changes in disposable income
- Changes in distribution of wealth
- Government policy
- Development of major new products
- Interest rates
- Price expectations

The business cycle

The **four main phases** of the **business cycle** are:

- **Recession (A)**
- **Depression (B)**
- **Recovery (C)**
- **Boom (D)**

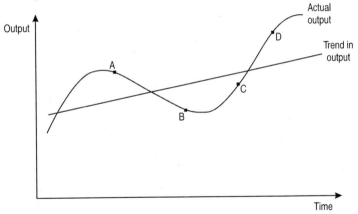

Inflation

An increase in price levels generally, and a decline in the purchasing power of money

Why is inflation a problem?

- Redistribution of income and wealth
- Balance of payments effects
- Price signalling and 'noise'
- Wage bargaining
- Consumer behaviour

Monetary policy

Government policies on the money supply, monetary system, interest rates, exchange rates and the availability of credit

Fiscal policy

Government policies on taxation, public borrowing and public spending

Supply-side policies

- Involve the private sector
- Reduce taxes
- Cut power of unions
- Improve education and training
- Increase competition
- Deregulate markets

11: The economic environment of business and finance

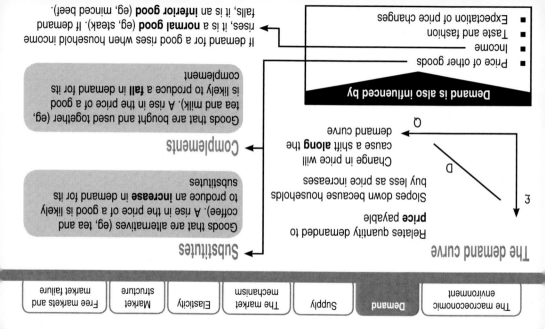

The demand curve

Relates quantity demanded to **price payable**

Slopes down because households buy less as price increases

Change in price will cause a shift **along** the demand curve

Substitutes

Goods that are alternatives (eg, tea and coffee). A rise in the price of a good is likely to produce an **increase** in demand for its substitutes

Complements

Goods that are bought and used together (eg, tea and milk). A rise in the price of a good is likely to produce a **fall** in demand for its complement

Demand is also influenced by

- Price of other goods
- Income
- Taste and fashion
- Expectation of price changes

If demand for a good rises when household income rises, it is a **normal good** (eg, steak). If demand falls, it is an **inferior good** (eg, minced beef).

Remember! The demand curve shows how demand responds to a change in price and nothing else! Any change in the other factors that affect demand cause a shift in the position of the demand curve.

A leftward shift may be caused by

- A fall in household income
- A fall in the price of substitutes
- A rise in the price of complements
- A change in taste away from the good
- An expected fall in price

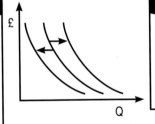

A rightward shift may be caused by

- A rise in household income
- A rise in the price of substitutes
- A fall in the price of complements
- A change in taste towards the good
- An expected rise in price

An expectation of a fall in price will lead consumers to put off their purchases in the hope of benefiting from the lower price later. An expected price rise will lead consumers to buy early and stockpile in order to avoid paying a higher price later.

11: The economic environment of business and finance

The supply curve

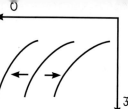

S

Relates quantity supplied to **price** payable

Slopes up because firms want to supply more if they can get a higher price

Change in price will cause a shift **along** the supply curve

---

Supply is also influenced by:

- Price of other goods
- Price of goods in joint supply
- Costs of making the item
- Changes in technology

Changes in these factors will cause a shift of the supply curve

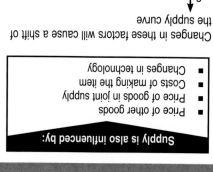

The market mechanism

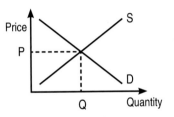

The market mechanism brings supply and demand together at the **equilibrium price** P. This is also the **market clearing price** since quantity Q is both offered and demanded and there is neither surplus nor shortage.

Functions of the market mechanism

- Market prices and their movements act as **signals** to producers, enabling them to produce what is most needed.
- When a firm operates efficiently, responding to market signals and controlling its costs, it receives a **reward** in the form of profit.
- The actions of firms in responding to the profit opportunities **allocate** resources to their best use.

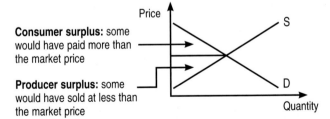

Consumer surplus: some would have paid more than the market price

Producer surplus: some would have sold at less than the market price

A shift of the demand or supply curve causes:
- A rise or fall in market price P
- An increase or decrease in quantity supplied Q

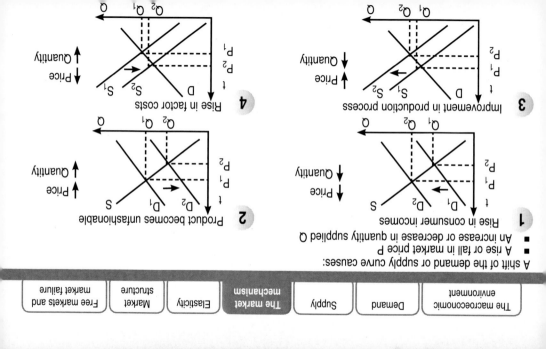

1 Rise in consumer incomes

2 Product becomes unfashionable

3 Improvement in production process

4 Rise in factor costs

Upward sloping demand curve

- Giffen goods – basic goods where a rise in price means the necessity of that purchase 'squeezes out' other items
- Veblen goods – goods bought for ostentation

Price regulation

Some governments attempt to overcome market forces by **regulating prices**

Maximum price

Used to combat inflation or make basic goods affordable

Minimum price

Used to secure incomes of favoured producers eg, farmers, oil

Price elasticity of demand (PED)

A measure of the change in **demand** for a good in response to a change in its **price**: when demand is **elastic** a small change in price produces a large change in demand. When the demand is inelastic, a large change in price produces only a small change in demand.

$$PED = \frac{\text{change in quantity demanded as \% of demand}}{\text{change in price as \% of price}} = \frac{\Delta Q}{Q} \times \frac{P}{\Delta P} = \frac{\Delta Q}{\Delta P} \times \frac{P}{Q}$$

P and Q may be values at a **point** or averages over an **arc**.

PED > 1 means that demand is elastic.

An increase in price from P_A to P_B leads to a fall in total expenditure.

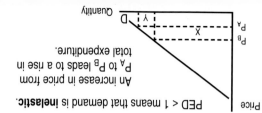

PED < 1 means that demand is inelastic.

An increase in price from P_A to P_B leads to a rise in total expenditure.

Factors affecting elasticity of supply

- Existence of inventory of all kinds of goods and their perishability
- Ease of adjusting labour inputs up or down
- Barriers to entry make supply inelastic
- Time scale ──

Factors affecting elasticity of demand

- Availability of substitutes
- Competitors pricing responses
- Necessities = inelastic, luxuries = elastic
- Percentage of income spent on a good – lower = more elastic
- Habit-forming goods = less elastic
- Time scale ──

Time factors

- Households may take a little time to respond to price but demand generally changes quicker than supply.
- During the **market period** only existing inventory and levels of output are available. Supply is **very inelastic.**
- Over the **short run**, quantities can be adjusted by working overtime or short time. Supply is **quite elastic.**
- Over the **long run** plant can be built or shut down. Supply is **very elastic.**

11: The economic environment of business and finance

Income elasticity of demand

How demand for a good changes in response to changes in household income

$$\frac{\text{\% change in quantity demanded}}{\text{\% change in household incomes}}$$

- >1 = income elastic → normal good
- <1 = income inelastic → inferior good

Price elasticity of supply

How supply responds to a change in price

$$\frac{\text{\% change in quantity supplied}}{\text{\% change in price}}$$

- 0 = perfectly inelastic → fixed supply
- 1 = unit elasticity → proportionate variation of supply with price
- ∞ = perfect elasticity → all is supplied at one price, none at any other price

Cross elasticity of demand

How demand for one good changes in response to a change in the price of another good (assuming no change in price of first good)

$$\frac{\text{\% change in quantity demanded of A}}{\text{\% change in price of B}}$$

- > 0 = positive cross-elasticity → substitutes
- < 0 = negative cross-elasticity → complements
- 0 = unrelated goods

Types of market structure

Perfect competition

- Many buyers/sellers who cannot influence the market price
- No entry/exit barriers
- Perfect information
- Homogenous products
- No collusion

Consequences

- Suppliers are price takers of the market-determined prices
- Normal profits
- Single selling price

Monopolistic competition

- Many buyers/sellers
- Branding and product differentiation
- Advertising and customer loyalty

Consequences

- Price rises

Oligopoly

- A few sellers, many buyers
- Differentiation
- Mutual interdependence

Consequences

- Price wars
- Cartels

Market structure

| The macroeconomic environment | Demand | Supply | The market mechanism | Elasticity | Market structure | Free markets and market failure |

Duopoly
- Two dominant sellers control prices

Consequences
- High prices
- Cartels

Types of monopoly
- Pure monopoly – only one supplier
- Actual monopoly – one dominant supplier
- Government franchise monopoly
- Natural monopoly – economies of scale

Monopoly
- One supplier, many buyers
- Barriers to entry

Consequences
- Monopoly **either** sets the market price **or** the quantity supplied
- Supernormal profits

Arguments for free markets

- Rapid adaptations to changing conditions
- Impersonal – price/output result from many individual decisions, not from regulation or central planning
- Efficient allocation of economic resources

Types of efficiency

- **Social efficiency** takes account of external costs and benefits
- **Allocative efficiency** – goods/services are produced at minimum cost
- **Technical efficiency** – goods/services are produced using minimum amount of resources
- **Productive efficiency** – all goods/services in economy are produced at lowest cost

Assumptions about free markets

- Large number of suppliers with a homogenous product and a small market share each
- Perfect information
- Perfect mobility of factors of production enabling switching
- Free entry to/exit from market

Market failure

Free market fails to allocate resources efficiently

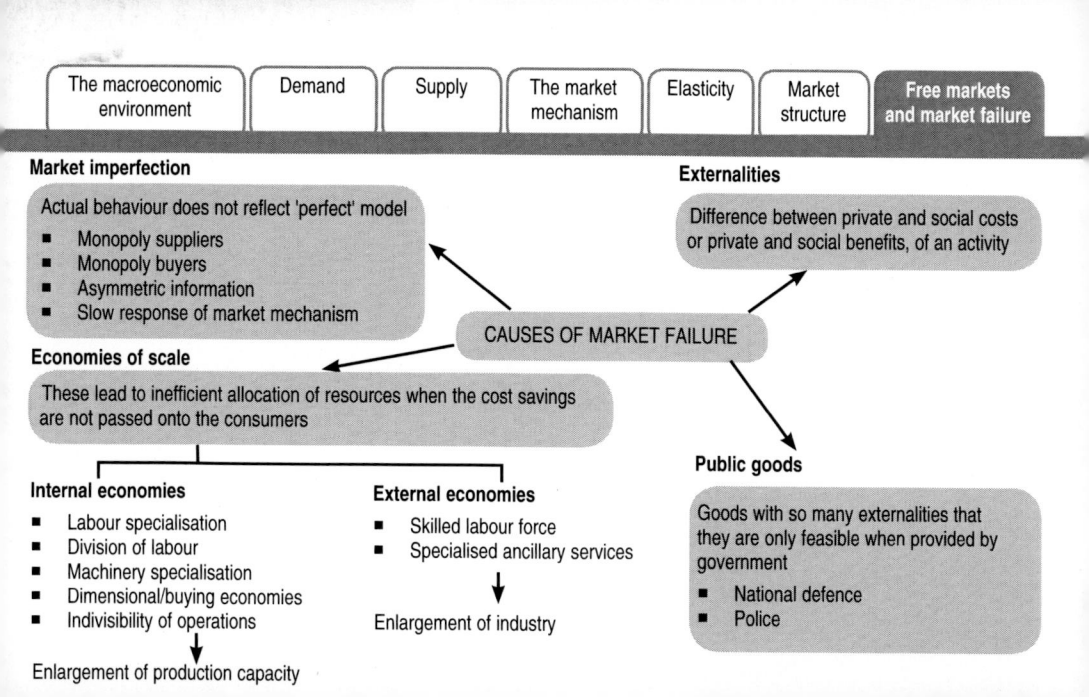

Market imperfection

Actual behaviour does not reflect 'perfect' model
- Monopoly suppliers
- Monopoly buyers
- Asymmetric information
- Slow response of market mechanism

Externalities

Difference between private and social costs or private and social benefits, of an activity

CAUSES OF MARKET FAILURE

Economies of scale

These lead to inefficient allocation of resources when the cost savings are not passed onto the consumers

Public goods

Goods with so many externalities that they are only feasible when provided by government
- National defence
- Police

Internal economies
- Labour specialisation
- Division of labour
- Machinery specialisation
- Dimensional/buying economies
- Indivisibility of operations

Enlargement of production capacity

External economies
- Skilled labour force
- Specialised ancillary services

Enlargement of industry

12: External regulation of business

In this chapter we cover how governments intervene in markets to address market failures, and to protect the public interest.

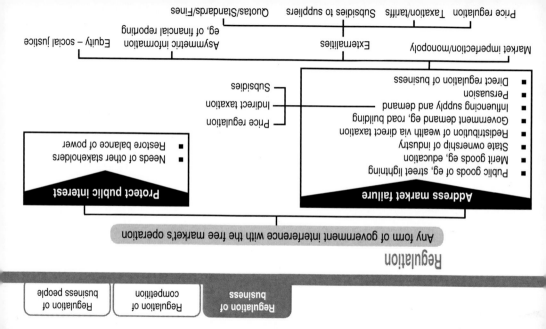

Potential responses of business

- **Entrenchment** – non-response
- **Mere compliance** – cost of compliance passed on to customers
- **Full compliance** – change in behaviour
- **Innovation** – the Porter hypothesis. Environmental regulation triggers discovery/introduction of cleaner technologies and environmental improvements

Efficient regulation: total benefits > total costs

Outcomes of business regulation

- Address market failure
- Change social standing of certain groups
- Implement desires of majority
- Increase diversity
- Deal with irreversibility

Regulatory bodies

- FRC
- Information Commission
- Competition and Markets Authority (CMA)

Regulation of business	**Regulation of competition**	Regulation of business people

Aim: To prevent the concentration of power in one or two suppliers. Maximum fine for breaching prohibitions 10% worldwide revenue.

1 Prohibition of anti-competitive agreements

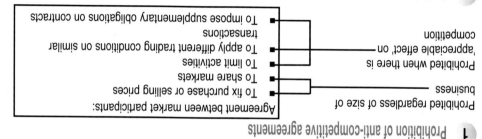

Prohibited regardless of size of business

Prohibited when there is 'appreciable effect' on competition

Agreement between market participants:
- To fix purchase or selling prices
- To share markets
- To limit activities
- To apply different trading conditions on similar transactions
- To impose supplementary obligations on contracts

2 Prohibition of abuse of dominant position → One where business can behave independently of competitive pressures

3 Prohibition of cartels

Cartel: agreement between businesses not to compete with each other

Cartels usually collude on:

- Prices
- Output levels
- Discounts and credit/terms
- Technology
- 'Carving up' markets geographically
- Bid rigging

More likely where:

- Few competitors
- Homogenous products
- Established communications between competitors
- Excess capacity
- An economic recession

Competition and Markets Authority

- May investigate when one firm controls the market or when a merger involves a large amount of assets worldwide
- It reports to the government
- It seeks to promote consumer interests, competition, enterprise and efficiency
- It tries to balance rewards for innovation and the benefits of scale economies against the disadvantages of monopoly

Competition and Markets Authority (continued)

- Powers of investigation
- Imposes penalties
- Can make Competition Disqualification Orders

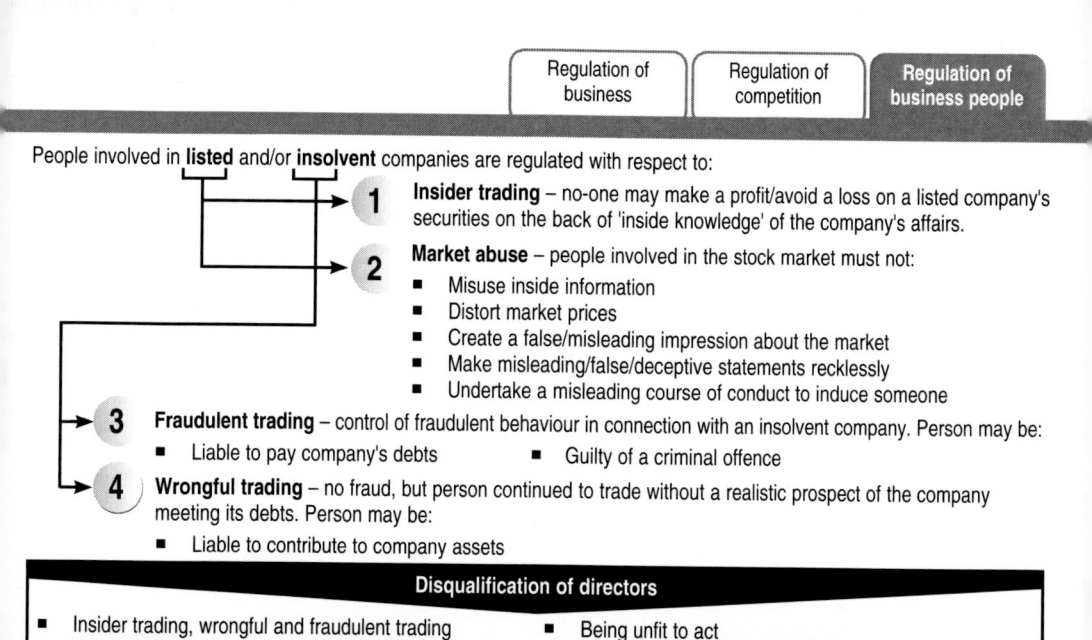

People involved in **listed** and/or **insolvent** companies are regulated with respect to:

1 **Insider trading** – no-one may make a profit/avoid a loss on a listed company's securities on the back of 'inside knowledge' of the company's affairs.

2 **Market abuse** – people involved in the stock market must not:
- Misuse inside information
- Distort market prices
- Create a false/misleading impression about the market
- Make misleading/false/deceptive statements recklessly
- Undertake a misleading course of conduct to induce someone

3 **Fraudulent trading** – control of fraudulent behaviour in connection with an insolvent company. Person may be:
- Liable to pay company's debts
- Guilty of a criminal offence

4 **Wrongful trading** – no fraud, but person continued to trade without a realistic prospect of the company meeting its debts. Person may be:
- Liable to contribute to company assets

Disqualification of directors

- Insider trading, wrongful and fraudulent trading
- Being the director of an insolvent company
- Being unfit to act
- Being a threat to the public interest

13: Data analysis

In this chapter we look at how information is used in business, including qualities of information, types of data analysis and potential problems with data.

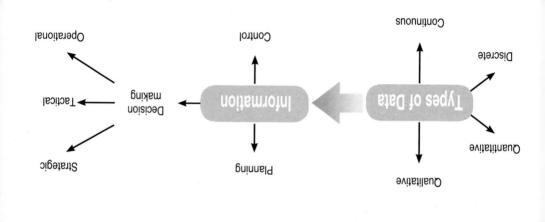

Qualities of good information: ACCURATE

Accurate: Adding-up, rounding, error-free, properly categorised, state assumptions, identify uncertainty

Complete: Include everything needed, such as external data, comparatives

Cost-beneficial: Benefits of having information > costs of obtaining it; efficient collection and analysis

User-targeted: Needs of user should be met eg, detailed or summarised?

Relevant: Unnecessary information should be omitted

Authoritative: Reliable sources

Timely: Should be available when it is needed

Easy to use: Clear presentation; no longer than necessary; sent in appropriate form, medium and channel

13: Data analysis

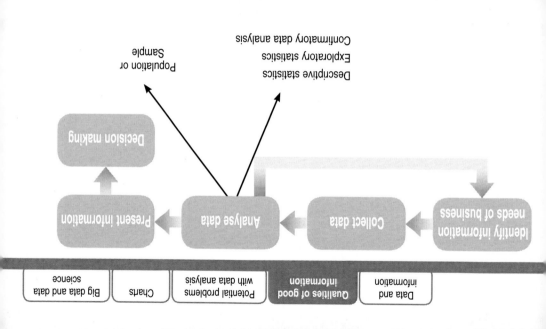

Professional scepticism: assessing information, estimates and explanations **critically** with a **questioning mind**, and **being alert to possible misstatements** due to error and fraud

Comparability: data not distorted by use of different definitions or measuring methods

Data bias: data in a sample is **not representative of the population**

- Selection bias
- Self-selection bias
- Observer bias
- Omitted variable bias
- Cognitive bias
- Survivorship bias

Type I error – a **hypothesis is true** but is **rejected** because the sample result differs significantly from hypothesis

Type II error – a **hypothesis is false** but is **accepted** because the sample result is not significantly different from hypothesis.

Bar Charts

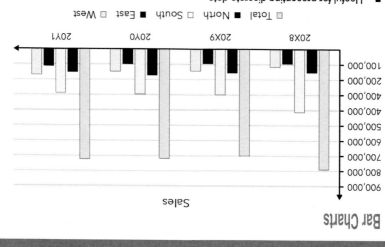

Sales

Legend: ☐ Total ■ North ☐ South ■ East ☐ West

- Useful for presenting discrete data
- Useful for comparisons between data sets (eg, sales by region)

Pie charts

Sales

- Useful for showing components that make up a total
- Not useful for more than one period

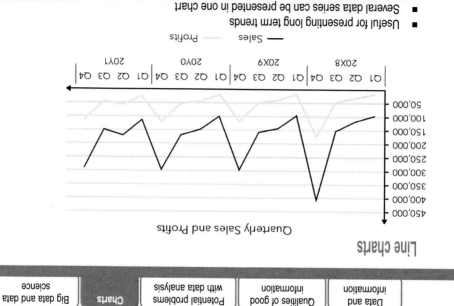

Line charts

Quarterly Sales and Profits

—— Sales   —— Profits

- Useful for presenting long term trends
- Several data series can be presented in one chart

| Data and information | Qualities of good information | Potential problems with data analysis | Charts | Big data and data science |

Big data

Datasets whose size is beyond the ability of typical database software to capture, store, manage and analyse.

Characteristics of big data

- Volume
- Velocity
- Variety
- Veracity

Risks of big data, data science and data analytics

- Storage
- Workforce skills
- Data dependency
- Information overload
- Data privacy
- Data security

Data science

Data science covers the whole life cycle of data, from acquisition and exploration to analysis and communication of the results. It is not only concerned with the tools and methods to obtain, manage and analyse data; it is also about extracting value from data and translating it from asset to product.

Data analytics

The process of collecting, organising and analysing large sets of data to discover patterns and other useful information which an organisation can use for its future business decisions.

14: Developments in technology

Topic List

Information systems

Technology and the accountancy profession

Cyber security and resilience

This final chapter examines some recent developments in technology and examines how they impact on the accountancy profession.

| Information systems | Technology and the accountancy profession | Cyber security and resilience |

Information system

All systems and procedures involved in the collection, storage, production and distribution of information

Data	Processing	Information
Complete range of new facts relating to events in the business or its environment	Collecting and conversion of data	Output of the information processing system

Sources of data

Internal
- Accounting records
- HR + payroll records
- Machine logs and operations/production control systems
- Procurement data systems
- Time sheets
- Staff

External
- Formal – legislation, regulation, research
- Informal – word-of-mouth, internet, newspapers, news agencies, libraries
- Internet of things

Effective processing: CATIVA

- Completeness
- Accuracy — Data should remain true to its sources
- Timeliness — Real-time
- Inalterability — No unauthorised intervention in
- Verifiability — Processing, or alteration on completion
- Accessibility — Follow through data trail to sources
  – Processing effectiveness should be open to scrutiny

Internet and social media

Businesses increasingly obtain data from internet and social media eg, about trends in the market.

Transaction processing system (TPS)

Performs, records and processes routine transactions

Executive support system (ESS) or Executive information system (EIS)

A sophisticated database that pools data from internal and external sources and makes information available to senior managers in an easy-to-use form. ESS help senior managers make strategic, unstructured decisions

Decision support system (DSS)

Combines data and analytical models or data analysis tools to support semi-structured and unstructured decision making

Office automation systems (OAS)

Systems that increase the productivity of data and information workers

Knowledge work systems (KWS)

Facilitate the creation and integration of new knowledge into an organisation

Management information system (MIS)

Converts internal data into information for managers to plan, control, organise and lead the business

Expert system

This captures human expertise in a limited domain of knowledge to allow users to benefit from expert knowledge and information. The system will consist of a database holding specialised data and rules about what to do in, or how to interpret, a given set of circumstances.

Distributed ledger technology

Distributed ledger technology allows multiple organisations to access an accurate, immutable shared record, that provides clarity about ownership of assets and existence of obligations and facilitates the transfer of ownership of assets.

Machine learning

Machine learning involves the use of machines to analyse large data sets of historic data to identify patterns and intelligence.

Digital assets

A digital asset is any text or media file or that is formatted into a binary source and that includes the right to use it; digital files that do not carry this right are not considered digital assets.

Automation

Automation is the creation of technology and its application in order to control and monitor the production and delivery of goods and services.

Cloud computing

A model for enabling ubiquitous, convenient, on-demand network access to a shared pool of configurable computing resources (eg, networks, servers, storage, applications, and services) that can be rapidly provisioned and released with minimal management effort or service provider interaction.

Cloud accounting

An application of cloud computing. Accountancy software is provided in the cloud by a service provider. The user accesses this software to process their accounting transactions and run reports as they would if the software was installed on their own computer.

Artificial intelligence (AI)

The use of computers to do tasks which are thought to require human intelligence. It typically refers to tasks such as learning, knowing, sensing, reasoning, creating things, problem-solving and generating and understanding language. Machine learning is a type of artificial intelligence.

Impacts of technology on the accountancy profession

The following two tables show how technology has impacted both accountants and auditors.

Technology development	Impact on accounting
Automation, machine learning and artificial intelligence	Maintaining ledgers and preparing reconciliations is no longer performed by humans.
More powerful systems	Processing speeds increase freeing up the accountant to perform value-adding roles.
System innovations and applications	Accountants required to provide advice on the adoption of innovations and how to use and account for them.
Digital contracts and transactions	Accountants are involved in new ways of recording transactions.
New types of data, information and risks	Increased need for sound judgement in accountants.
New types of goods and services	Accountants to advise clients and employees on how to account for items arising from new technology such as digital assets.
Transparency in recording and sharing data	Distributed ledgers, for instance, mean there is more clarity about resources due to the improved recording of transactions.

Technology development	Impact on auditing
Audit analytics and intelligent systems	New systems allow complete checks on data and allow 100% of transactions to be audited automatically on a continuous basis.
Smart contracts	The audit of smart contracts to take place as the smart contract is being created, before transactions under it occur.
Data analytics	Predictive analytics helps to target risk and improves the relevance of audits.
Software controls and data sets	Audit work to focus on validating controls within the accounting software and on interpreting complex data sets.
Innovations such as distributed ledger technology and advanced accounting systems	Properly functioning distributed ledgers and software reduce the need for auditors to audit transactions and verify the ownership of assets.
Regulation	Audit regulations must adapt to technological developments.

Cyber security

Cyber risk - loss, disruption or reputational damage from failure of IT systems due to accidents, breach of security, cyber-attacks or poor systems integrity

Cyber-attack: A **deliberate action** through the Internet against an organisation **with the intention of causing loss, damage or disruption to activities.**

Hacking	Using specialist software and tools to gain unauthorised access to systems
Phishing	Using bogus emails to obtain security information (eg, passwords)
Hijack/ransomware	Criminals hijack files and hold them to ransom
Keylogging	Criminals record what the user types into their computer
Distributed denial of service attack (DDOS)	Overwhelming an organisation's website with a wave of internet traffic designed to crash the systems

Controls to reduce the risk of a cyber-attack:

- Firewalls
- Secure systems configurations
- Access controls (physical and logical)
- Malware and virus protection
- Install software updates regularly

Cyber resilience

Cyber resilience: ability to ensure that data and information are **reliable, available,** has **integrity** and is adequately **protected from unauthorised access.**

ICAEW report "Developing a cyber-resilience strategy:" Identifies **specific risks to cyber security:**

Mobile threats - data is held on mobile devices which could be lost

Networking and cloud considerations - connections to internet go down

Access controls - inferior access controls on mobile devices

Report suggests an information security plan to cover these risks.